W9-COM-651

The Cardamom Trail

The Cardamom Trail

Chetna Bakes with Flavours of the East

Chetna Makan

MITCHELL BEAZLEY

SOMERSET CO. LIBRARY
BRIDGEWATER, N.J. 08807

For Sia, Yuv and Gaurav

An Hachette UK Company
www.hachette.co.uk

First published in Great Britain in 2016
by Mitchell Beazley, a division of Octopus
Publishing Group Ltd, Carmelite House,
50 Victoria Embankment,
London EC4Y 0DZ
www.octopusbooks.co.uk

Text copyright © Chetna Makan 2016
Design and layout copyright © Octopus
Publishing Group Ltd 2016

Distributed in the US by Hachette Book Group,
1290 Avenue of the Americas, 4th and 5th
Floors, New York, NY 10020

Distributed in Canada by Canadian Manda
Group, 664 Annette St, Toronto, Ontario,
Canada M6S 2C8

All rights reserved. No part of this work may
be reproduced or utilized in any form or by
any means, electronic or mechanical, including
photocopying, recording or by any information
storage and retrieval system, without the prior
written permission of the publisher.

Chetna Makan asserts the moral right to be
identified as the author of this work.

ISBN 978 1 78472 129 9

A CIP catalogue record for this book is
available from the British Library.

Printed and bound in China

10 9 8 7 6 5 4 3 2 1

Commissioning Editor Eleanor Maxfield
Art Director Juliette Norsworthy
Senior Editor Leanne Bryan
Designer Lizzie Ballantyne
Copy Editor Salima Hirani
Photographer Nassima Rothacker
Food and Prop Stylist Polly Webb-Wilson
Illustrator Grace Helmer
Assistant Production Manager Caroline Alberti

Contents

Introduction

The Cardamom Trail is about my culinary journey so far. It brings together all my food memories in the shape of lovely bakes and new taste sensations. Within this cookbook you'll find traditional bakes inspired by Indian food as well as some modern spice-inspired recipes. Brits are well known for their love of Indian food and, in my experience, they're already familiar with a wide range of Asian ingredients – chillies and chickpeas, turmeric and tamarind, poppy seeds and paneer. These wonderful flavours are all readily available in supermarkets and Asian grocery stores these days, yet few people think of using them in baking. I want to encourage you to do that, to experiment as I do and give your favourite bakes a new edge. Indian spices can transform your baking, whether it's a sponge cake with cardamom, pistachio and white chocolate (*see* page 39), steamed strawberry pudding flavoured with cinnamon (*see* page 113), coriander chicken parcels (*see* page 157) or a swirly bread rolled with citrusy coriander (*see* page 193). My pies, for instance, are filled with time-honoured recipes I have known since childhood – you just wouldn't normally find them in a hot water crust!

I've eaten good home-cooked food for as long as I can remember. Growing up in Jabalpur, an ancient city in the state of Madhya Pradesh in Central India, there was almost no processed food, nor did we eat out often. My mother cooked all our meals from scratch – everything from simple suppers to elaborate festive feasts – always using fresh, raw ingredients. Often she would make up the dish as she cooked it. She didn't follow recipes, although she was and remains a keen learner – I still see her scribbling new ideas in her diary. Watching Mum work her magic in the kitchen inspired my love of cooking. I'm a keen learner, too. Observing her skilled use of spices and other ingredients gave me the confidence to mix flavours and try new ideas.

Home baking is not very popular in India and, as with most Indian kitchens, ours did not have a built-in oven. Most home cooking is done on the hob, and in restaurants the oven of choice is the tandoor. My first memories of baking are of Mum using our very basic tabletop oven (which she still uses) to make birthday cakes for my two sisters and me. As I grew older,

I would bake cakes myself for friends and my many cousins – we had a large extended family and there was always plenty of great food at family gatherings, celebrations and festivals. We regularly visited local bakeries for treats such as cream rolls, pineapple cake, rum balls, doughnuts and *pattice* (savoury puff pastry snacks) – just thinking of these transports me home. Whenever I return to India, I make a point of visiting the old bakeries to relive those wonderful moments from my childhood. The shops still make the same bakes, even after all these years, and I have recreated some of them for this book.

I always wanted to pursue arts and a creative profession, so I left home at 17 to study at Mumbai's National Institute of Fashion Technology, NIFT. Mumbai is a sprawling, multicultural city with all manner of food influences. Living there exposed me to a completely different kind of Indian cuisine than the one I was used to at home in Jabalpur, 700 miles away. The spices and their uses were distinct, and the street food was amazing. I cooked my way through my student life, even though the kitchen facilities were basic at best. I also spent a lot of time with the lovely Pereira family who, being Goan Catholics, had their own special ways of cooking. Patricia, the lady of the house, made the best biryani, fish curries and sugar-crusted doughnuts. Looking back, I can see that although my baking came to a complete halt during this time, my understanding of flavours grew tremendously and influenced the way I cook and bake today.

After graduation, I worked as a fashion designer for five years in Mumbai. My work involved international travel to countries like France, Italy, America and the UK. Even though my stay in these places was usually very short, my love of good food ensured that I tried different cuisines as much as I could.

In 2004, I moved with my husband to the small seaside town of Broadstairs in Kent. It was quite a shock after cosmopolitan Mumbai. I missed the excitement and buzz of a big city, but soon fell in love with the natural beauty and relaxed pace of life. That was when I discovered Victoria sponge! I'd never before seen or tasted this humble yet undoubtedly wonderful concoction of cake, strawberry jam and fresh cream. It remains my favourite.

I tentatively returned to baking when I had children – once again, it was birthday cakes that got me going. I began looking for new recipes. Although I loved traditional bakes, I wanted to add my own flavours and creativity – I was missing my work as a designer and baking was the perfect creative outlet. Around that time a new television show, *The Great British Bake Off*, caught my attention and introduced me to many amazing bakes. Soon I was making cakes for friends and coffee mornings, and, one day, at my friends' insistence, I applied to go on the programme. Of course, I never expected anything to result from my application, but a few months later I found myself in a big white tent amid people who had been baking for years.

When I started practising to take part in *Bake Off*, I discovered that many classic European bakes taste a bit similar, at least to my palate. This led me to think of infusing my recipes with Indian flavours to set them apart. Throughout the competition I threw in a spice here or a herb there to give my recipes an unusual twist. This seemed to be appreciated by the judges and my fellow bakers, and helped me reach the semi-final. My whole *Bake Off* experience was amazing; I learned so much about baking and made some wonderful friends. It gave me the confidence to go further and to commit to building a career in food, pairing my knowledge of spices and flavours with traditional bakes to create extraordinary dishes and treats. And in this book I have gathered the best of my recipes to date.

To make the most of this book, explore the side dishes and accompaniments, for I believe they will make your meals truly memorable. I like to eat savoury bakes with something on the side, such as a tart with a salad. Chutneys make finger food more special, and raita goes perfectly with stuffed naan. Don't be afraid to mix and match the recipes here – you could spoon Cucumber Raita (*see* page 232) over the Aubergine and Onion Tart (*see* page 88), serve Rajma Paratha (*see* page 204) with Coconut Paneer (*see* page 199), or try Boondi Raita (*see* page 235) with Dal Kachori (*see* page 173).

Take the same approach with the cakes and pastries: pair the icings that catch your attention with different cakes to those in the recipes according to your own tastes, and add your favourite fruits to the fillings. The Showstopper Victoria Sponge (*see* page 35) would be lovely with passion fruit curd, and you could add slivers of apricot to my jam-filled mini meringue cakes (*see* page 99).

All the recipes within this baking book have been part of my life at one time or another and I hope that, being grounded in the different cuisines of India and Europe, they epitomize the best of both worlds. Please enjoy this book and use it as a springboard for your own creativity.

Cakes

I love the flavour balance in this cake: tangy pears, floral cardamom, rich caramel and, underneath, a moist sponge of orange and almonds. Do try it – your friends and family will think it a triumph.

Pear and cardamom caramel upside-down cake

Serves 12–14

150g (5½oz) caster sugar

200g (7oz) unsalted butter, softened, plus extra for greasing

150g (5½oz) self-raising flour

50g (1¾oz) ground almonds

1 teaspoon baking powder

4 large eggs

finely grated zest of 2 oranges

For the topping

50g (1¾oz) unsalted butter

100g (3½oz) light muscovado sugar

1 teaspoon ground cardamom

4 pears, peeled, cored and halved

Preheat the oven to 180°C (350°F), Gas Mark 4. Grease a 23cm (9in) round springform cake tin.

First, make the topping. In a saucepan, gently heat the butter, sugar and ground cardamom until the sugar has dissolved and the butter has melted. Cook for 2 minutes, stirring often. Pour this sauce carefully into the prepared tin and spread it evenly over the base. Sit the halved pears in it with the cut sides facing down.

To make the cake, put all the ingredients in a large bowl and mix with an electric whisk for 2 minutes until light and creamy. Carefully spoon this mixture over the pears, taking care not to disturb them, then bake for 50–55 minutes until a skewer inserted into the centre of the cake comes out clean. Leave to cool in the tin for 10 minutes, then carefully turn out on to a wire rack. Enjoy warm or cold. The cake will keep in an airtight container for up to 4 days.

In this recipe, I have brought together three of my favourite ingredients in a lovely celebration cake that looks beautiful sitting on a dinner table. The freshness of this flavour combination is also perfect for alfresco dining in summer.

Mango, cardamom and coconut cake

Serves 8–10

For the cake

200g (7oz) unsalted butter, softened, plus extra for greasing

175g (6oz) golden caster sugar

200g (7oz) self-raising flour

1 teaspoon baking powder

1 teaspoon ground cardamom

4 large eggs

40g (1½oz) desiccated coconut

2 tablespoons coconut cream

For the filling and decoration

300g (10½oz) double cream

200g (7oz) mascarpone cheese

4 tablespoons caster sugar

2 mangoes, stoned and peeled

Preheat the oven to 180°C (350°F), Gas Mark 4. Grease 2 × 18cm (7in) round cake tins and line with nonstick baking paper.

In a large bowl, combine the butter, sugar, flour, baking powder, ground cardamom and eggs and mix with an electric whisk for 2 minutes or until light and creamy. Fold in the desiccated coconut and coconut cream. Divide the batter evenly between the prepared tins and bake for 20–25 minutes or until a skewer inserted into the centre of the cakes comes out clean. Leave the cakes to cool in the tins.

To make the filling, whisk the cream, mascarpone and sugar in a bowl until the mixture is thick. Chop the flesh of 1 mango into small pieces and fold it into the cream. Cut the flesh of the other mango into thin strips or cubes, as desired.

To assemble, cut each cake horizontally into 2 equal layers. Place 1 layer on a serving plate and spread over it a quarter of the cream icing. Align another cake layer on top and repeat the layering process, ending with a layer of cream icing on the top of the cake. Decorate the top with the fresh mango strips or cubes and serve. This cake will keep, refrigerated, in an airtight container for up to 4 days. Leave to stand at room temperature for 30 minutes before serving.

Gulkand is a rose petal preserve that, in India, is served with betel leaves in *paan*, a spicy after-dinner mouth freshener that also aids digestion. This cake takes inspiration from that delicious combination. I love the way the aniseed kick of fennel balances the rosewater and adds subtlety to its flavour. The fennel seeds and dried rose petals give a nice bit of crunch to the layers of creamy icing and dense honey-and-almond cake.

Rose and honey cake

Serves 10–12

100g (3¹/₂oz) golden caster sugar

100g (3¹/₂oz) clear honey

100g (3¹/₂oz) self-raising flour

100g (3¹/₂oz) ground almonds

200g (7oz) unsalted butter, softened, plus extra for greasing

1 teaspoon baking powder

4 large eggs

1 teaspoon rosewater

For the rose mix

20g (³/₄oz) dried Indian rose petals

1 tablespoon dry-roasted fennel seeds

¹/₂ teaspoon ground cardamom

4 tablespoons caster sugar

For the icing

300ml (¹/₂ pint) double cream

2 tablespoons caster sugar

1 tablespoon dry-roasted fennel seeds, lightly crushed

Preheat the oven to 180°C (350°F), Gas Mark 4. Grease 2 × 20cm (8in) cake tins and line them with nonstick baking paper.

In a large bowl, mix all the cake ingredients with an electric whisk for 2 minutes until light and creamy. Pour the batter equally into the prepared tins and bake for 20–25 minutes or until a skewer inserted in the centre of the cakes comes out clean. Leave the cakes to cool in the tins for 10 minutes, then turn out on to a wire rack and leave to cool completely.

To make the rose mix, combine all the ingredients in a saucepan and cook over a low heat for 2–3 minutes, stirring continuously. Take the pan off the heat as soon as the sugar starts to melt. Give it a good stir and set aside to cool.

To make the icing, whisk the cream and sugar together in a bowl until soft peaks form. Fold in the fennel seeds.

To assemble, place 1 cake on a serving plate and spread half the icing over it. Sprinkle with half the rose mix. Place the second cake on top. Spread the remaining icing over this layer and finish by sprinkling over the last of the rose mix. This cake will keep, refrigerated, in an airtight container for up to 4 days. Leave it to sit at room temperature for 10 minutes before serving.

I love the combination of almonds and coffee. Normally it is associated with rich desserts such as gâteau opéra, but in this cake the sponge is made with ground and flaked almonds, which makes it light. The richness comes with the buttery chocolate icing and can be topped with yet more almonds! You can buy bags of ready-toasted flaked almonds, or toast flaked almonds yourself in a dry frying pan – remember to keep stirring them over a low heat so that they brown evenly, and tip the toasted almonds into a bowl to cool rather than leave them in the hot frying pan once you've taken them off the heat to prevent scorching.

Almond and coffee cake

Serves 10–12

175g (6oz) unsalted butter, softened, plus extra for greasing

175g (6oz) golden caster sugar

3 large eggs

150g (5½oz) self-raising flour

½ teaspoon baking powder

50g (1¾oz) ground almonds

2 tablespoons milk

2 tablespoons coffee granules dissolved in 1 tablespoon boiling water

20g (¾oz) toasted flaked almonds, plus a handful extra to decorate (optional)

For the icing

35g (1¼oz) unsalted butter

100g (3½oz) icing sugar, sifted

1 tablespoon cocoa powder

2 tablespoons boiling water

Preheat the oven to 180°C (350°F), Gas Mark 4. Grease a bundt cake tin or any 25cm (10in) round or square cake tin.

Cream the butter and sugar together using an electric whisk or a stand mixer fitted with a paddle attachment until light and fluffy. Then add the eggs, 1 at a time, beating well after each addition. Now add the flour, baking powder, ground almonds, milk and dissolved coffee. Beat the mixture for 1 minute until well combined. Fold in the flaked almonds using a spatula or a large metal spoon.

Pour the batter into the prepared tin and bake for 35–40 minutes or until a skewer inserted into the centre of the cake comes out clean. Leave to cool in the tin for 10 minutes, then turn out on to a wire rack and leave to cool completely.

To make the icing, melt the butter in a small saucepan over a low heat, then take the pan off the heat and stir in the icing sugar. In a cup, stir the cocoa powder into the measured boiling water until dissolved, then add to the icing sugar mixture. Using a whisk, beat until the icing is smooth.

Pour the icing over the cooled cake and sprinkle the extra toasted flaked almonds on top, if liked. Store the cake in an airtight container for up to 5 days.

Coconut is used frequently to make sweets in India, and in this recipe I combine its fresh flavour with delicious chocolate. This luxurious cake is all about richness and texture. I use creamed coconut for a good consistency (coconut milk would be too runny and fresh coconut would not produce the creaminess we want here). The result is a very special cake that is perfect for a celebration.

Chocolate and coconut cake

Serves 8–10

150g (5½oz) unsalted butter, softened, plus extra for greasing

300g (10½oz) caster sugar

2 large eggs

1 teaspoon vanilla extract

250g (9oz) plain flour

50g (1¾oz) cocoa powder

pinch of salt

1 teaspoon bicarbonate of soda

150ml (¼ pint) buttermilk

150ml (¼ pint) boiling water

25g (1oz) creamed coconut

For the icing and decoration

250g (9oz) cream cheese

50g (1¾oz) unsalted butter, softened

50g (1¾oz) plain dark chocolate, melted

400g (14oz) icing sugar, sifted, plus more as needed

2 tablespoons coconut cream

1 teaspoon vanilla extract

60g (2¼oz) desiccated coconut

handful of coconut strips, toasted

Preheat the oven to 180°C (350°F), Gas Mark 4. Grease 2 × 20cm (8in) round cake tins and line them with nonstick baking paper.

Cream the butter and sugar together using an electric whisk or a stand mixer fitted with a paddle attachment until light and fluffy. Then add the eggs, 1 at a time, mixing well after each addition. Now mix in the vanilla extract.

In a separate bowl, mix the flour, cocoa powder, salt and bicarbonate of soda together. Add this to the egg mixture a couple of tablespoons at a time. After each addition, add a little of the buttermilk. Mix well.

In a jug, mix the measured boiling water with the creamed coconut. Slowly add this to the cake mix and whisk until the mixture is well combined.

Pour the batter equally into the prepared tins. Bake for 30–35 minutes or until a skewer inserted into the centre of the cake comes out clean. Leave to cool in the tins for 10 minutes, then turn the cakes out on to a wire rack and leave to cool completely.

To make the icing, beat the cream cheese and butter together in a large bowl until smooth. Mix in the melted chocolate, then slowly add the icing sugar, a little at a time, alternating this with additions of the coconut cream. Add the vanilla extract and mix well. Now add the desiccated coconut and lightly fold it in. If the icing is runny, add more icing sugar until it has a spreadable consistency.

Place 1 of the cakes on a serving plate. Spread some of the icing over the top. Align the second cake on top, then cover the stack with the icing and smooth it out. Arrange the toasted coconut strips on top of the cake to finish. This cake will keep, refrigerated, in an airtight container for up to 4 days. Leave to stand at room temperature for a few minutes before serving.

In this recipe, the world-renowned New York-style cheesecake gets a lavish Indian makeover. Rosewater and mint leaves make it fresh and fragrant, while the white chocolate adds extra dimensions of creaminess and richness. I like to include a little mascarpone in cheesecakes because it gives them a beautiful consistency.

Rose, mint and white chocolate cheesecake

Serves 14–16

225g (8oz) digestive biscuits

100g (3½oz) unsalted butter, melted, plus extra for greasing

150g (5½oz) white chocolate

600g (1lb 5oz) cream cheese

250g (9oz) mascarpone cheese

175g (6oz) caster sugar

2 large eggs

2 egg yolks

4 tablespoons plain flour

3 teaspoons rosewater

2 tablespoons mint leaves, finely chopped

For the topping and decoration

few rose petals

few mint sprigs

1 egg white, lightly beaten

3 tablespoons caster sugar

100g (3½oz) soured cream

Preheat the oven to 180°C (350°F), Gas Mark 4. Grease a 23cm (9in) springform cake tin and line it with nonstick baking paper.

Put the digestive biscuits in a plastic bag and bash with a rolling pin to crush them to fine crumbs. Mix with the melted butter and press the mixture into the prepared tin, using the back of a spoon to compress it into an even base layer. Bake for 10 minutes, then set aside to cool for 15 minutes.

Break the white chocolate into a heatproof bowl and set it over a pan of steaming water until melted, ensuring that the base of the bowl doesn't touch the water beneath it. Leave to cool slightly.

Put the cream cheese, mascarpone, sugar, whole eggs and yolks, flour, rosewater and mint in a large bowl and whisk until well combined. Add the melted chocolate and whisk well until smooth.

Pour this mixture over the biscuit base and bake for 35–40 minutes until the surface of the cheesecake has a uniform wobble. Turn off the oven and leave the cake inside it until completely cool.

Meanwhile, brush the rose petals and mint sprigs with a thin layer of egg white and dip them in the caster sugar. Leave them to dry for a couple of hours.

Remove the cheesecake from the tin, spread the soured cream on top and decorate with the rose petals and crystallized mint sprigs. This cake will keep, refrigerated, in an airtight container for up to 3 days.

I am not very fond of carrot cake, which is why I add banana for extra moistness and a few spices to cheer it up! Walnuts are, of course, a classic inclusion.

Carrot and banana spiced cake

Serves 10–12

200g (7oz) unsalted butter, softened, plus extra for greasing

200g (7oz) light soft brown sugar

200g (7oz) carrots, grated

1 ripe banana, mashed

1 teaspoon ground cinnamon

1 teaspoon ground cardamom

200g (7oz) self-raising flour

1 teaspoon baking powder

4 eggs, separated

50g (1³/₄oz) walnuts, roughly chopped

For the icing and decoration

250g (9oz) mascarpone cheese

2 tablespoons icing sugar, sifted

handful of walnuts, roughly chopped

Preheat the oven to 180°C (350°F), Gas Mark 4. Grease a deep 22–25cm (8½–10in) square cake tin and line it with nonstick baking paper.

Cream the sugar and butter together until light and fluffy. Add the grated carrot, mashed banana, cinnamon and cardamom and mix well. Then add the flour, baking powder and egg yolks and mix well again.

In a large bowl, whisk the egg whites until soft peaks form. Fold this into the cake batter, adding the walnuts. Pour the batter into the prepared tin and bake for 45–50 minutes or until a skewer inserted into the centre of the cake comes out clean. Leave to cool in the tin for 10 minutes, then turn out on to a wire rack and leave to cool completely.

To make the icing, beat the mascarpone and icing sugar together to a smooth paste, then spoon the mixture over the cooled cake and spread it over the surface with a palette knife. Sprinkle the chopped walnuts on top to serve. This cake will keep, refrigerated, in an airtight container for up to 4 days. If you have not iced the cake, it is better stored in an airtight container at room temperature.

These lovely light cakes are perfect for those parties for which you have lots of friends and family over. The spicy sweetness of cinnamon balances the sharpness of orange perfectly, and the rich creaminess of the mascarpone icing is divine. You don't have to use a piping bag to put the batter into the cake tin, but I highly recommend it any time you are making small cakes or filling small holes, as it makes the mixture much easier to handle for such fiddly jobs.

Orange and cinnamon mini cakes

Makes 12

190g (6½oz) unsalted butter, softened, plus extra for greasing

190g (6½oz) golden caster sugar

190g (6½oz) self-raising flour

3 large eggs

finely grated zest of 4 oranges

For the icing

300ml (½ pint) double cream

200g (7oz) mascarpone cheese

1 teaspoon ground cinnamon

2 tablespoons golden caster sugar

100g (3½oz) pistachio nuts

For the candied peel

1 orange

75g (2¾oz) caster sugar, plus extra for coating

splash of water

Preheat the oven to 180°C (350°F), Gas Mark 4. Grease a 12-hole mini brownie tin. If you don't have a mini cake tin with rectangular recesses, use a 12-hole muffin tin.

Put all the cake ingredients in a large bowl and mix with an electric whisk for 2 minutes until the mixture becomes light and creamy. Fill a disposable piping bag with the batter, cut off the tip and pipe it into the recesses of the prepared tin. Bake for 20 minutes or until done. Leave the mini cakes to cool in the tin for 10 minutes, then turn out on to a wire rack and leave to cool completely.

While the cakes are cooling, prepare the icing. Whisk the cream and mascarpone cheese with the ground cinnamon and sugar until stiff peaks form. Chop the pistachios finely.

Using a serrated knife, level the tops of the cakes, then slice each cake horizontally into 2 equal halves.

For the candied peel, remove a thin layer of the skin from the orange with a vegetable peeler and slice it into fine strips with a sharp knife. Melt the sugar with the water in a small saucepan over a low heat. Bring to the boil and simmer until a thick syrup is formed or the mixture reaches thread stage. Remove the syrup from the heat and add the strips of peel. Leave them to soak in the hot syrup for about 1 minute, then remove them with a slotted spoon and arrange on a baking tray lined with nonstick baking paper to cool. Sprinkle a layer of caster sugar over the cooled strips of peel and toss to coat.

Fill a clean disposable piping bag with the cream icing, cut off the tip and pipe it on to the lower halves of the mini cakes, then align the upper halves on top. Pipe some more cream icing on to the tops of the sandwiched cakes, then sprinkle the chopped pistachios and candied peel over the tops. These mini cakes will keep, refrigerated, in an airtight container for up to 4 days. Leave them to sit at room temperature for a few minutes before serving.

Decorate this dessert cake as simply or as lavishly as you like. It is great for celebrations – the classic combination of chocolate and orange, but with a surprising kick of chilli. If you are not a fan of chilli, feel free to leave it out – the cake will still be utterly delicious.

Chilli and chocolate mousse cake

Serves 10–12

200g (7oz) unsalted butter, softened, plus extra for greasing

200g (7oz) caster sugar

200g (7oz) self-raising flour

1 teaspoon baking powder

4 large eggs

finely grated zest of 3 oranges

For the syrup

4 tablespoons caster sugar

4 tablespoons water

4 tablespoons orange liqueur

For the mousse

125g (4^1/$_2$oz) plain dark chocolate (70 per cent cocoa solids)

125g (4^1/$_2$oz) milk chocolate

^{1}/$_2$ teaspoon chilli powder

4 large eggs

85g (3oz) caster sugar

For the decoration

200ml (^{1}/$_3$ pint) double cream

chocolate curls or cocoa powder

Preheat the oven to 180°C (350°F), Gas Mark 4. Grease 2 × 20cm (8in) cake tins and line them with nonstick baking paper.

Put all the cake ingredients in a large bowl and mix with an electric whisk for 2 minutes until the mixture is light and creamy. Pour the batter equally into the prepared tins and bake for 20–25 minutes or until a skewer inserted in the centre of the cakes comes out clean. Leave to cool in the tins for 10 minutes, then turn out on to a wire rack and leave to cool completely.

To make the syrup, combine all the ingredients in a saucepan and bring to the boil, stirring occasionally. Once the sugar has dissolved, turn off the heat and leave the syrup to cool.

To make the mousse, break both types of chocolate into a heatproof bowl and set the bowl over a pan of steaming water until the chocolate has melted, ensuring that the base of the bowl doesn't touch the water beneath it. Once melted, stir in the chilli powder and leave to cool for 5 minutes.

Separate the eggs into 2 large mixing bowls. Whisk the egg yolks with the sugar until very pale and creamy. Add the melted chocolate and fold together.

In another bowl, whisk the egg whites until they form soft peaks. Gradually fold the egg whites into the chocolate mixture until well incorporated.

Line a deep 20cm (8in) springform cake tin with clingfilm. Cut each cake in half horizontally so that you have 4 equal layers. Place 1 layer in the cake tin and brush the top with some of the syrup. Cover with one-third of the chilli-chocolate mousse. Repeat this layering process twice more, then add the last cake layer, keeping it plain on top. Cover the lot with clingfilm and chill for 2–3 hours or, preferably, overnight.

Once the cake is set, take off the clingfilm, carefully remove it from the tin and place it on a serving plate. To decorate the cake, whisk the cream until soft peaks form. Spread the cream on top of the cake. Decorate with chocolate curls or with a simple sprinkling of cocoa powder to serve. This cake will keep, refrigerated, in an airtight container for up to 4 days.

Victoria sponge is my favourite cake ever – my introduction to British baking, in fact – so I had to include one in this book. My take on this simple classic is to use a quick homemade berry jam and lemon curd to elevate it to showstopper status.

Showstopper Victoria sponge

Serves 6–8

200g (7oz) unsalted butter, softened, plus extra for greasing

200g (7oz) caster sugar

200g (7oz) self-raising flour

1 teaspoon baking powder

1 tablespoon milk

$^1/_2$ teaspoon vanilla bean paste

4 large eggs

For the jam

150g (5$^1/_2$oz) raspberries

100g (3$^1/_2$oz) strawberries, hulled

200g (7oz) caster sugar

1 tablespoon lemon juice

For the lemon curd

finely grated zest and juice of 4 lemons

100g (3$^1/_2$oz) unsalted butter, diced

225g (8oz) caster sugar

4 eggs

4 egg yolks

For the cream

400ml (14fl oz) double cream

2 tablespoons caster sugar

Preheat the oven to 180°C (350°F), Gas Mark 4. Grease 5 × 15cm (6in) round cake tins and line them with nonstick baking paper. (If you don't have 15cm/6in cake tins, use 2 × 20cm/8in cake tins and divide each of these cakes into 2 layers, then assemble the cake with 4 layers instead of 5.)

To make the sponge, use an electric whisk to whisk all the cake ingredients together in a large bowl for 2 minutes or until the mixture becomes light and creamy. Spoon the batter equally into the prepared tins and bake for 12–15 minutes (or for 20–25 minutes, if using 20cm/8in cake tins) or until a skewer inserted in the centre of the cakes comes out clean. Leave the cakes to cool in the tins for 10 minutes, then turn out on to a wire rack and leave to cool completely.

Meanwhile, prepare the jam. Combine all the ingredients in a saucepan and bring to the boil. Cook over the high heat for 10–15 minutes until the jam thickens enough to coat the back of a spoon. Tip it into a bowl and set aside to cool.

To make the lemon curd, put the lemon zest and juice, butter and sugar in a saucepan and heat over a low heat until the sugar and butter have melted. In a bowl, whisk the whole eggs and yolks together. Over a very low heat, slowly add the whole eggs to the saucepan, whisking continuously. Cook very gently for 5–10 minutes until thick, then strain through a sieve into a bowl and set aside to cool.

To prepare the cream, whisk the double cream with the caster sugar in a bowl until soft peaks form.

To assemble, place a cake layer on a serving plate and spread some of the cream over the top. Add a couple of tablespoons of lemon curd and spread evenly. Cover with another cake layer and spread with cream. This time, spread jam on top of the cream. (Any leftover jam and curd will keep, refrigerated, in an airtight container for up to 3–4 weeks.) Now repeat with all the layers, alternating the curd and jam. Once the cake tower is ready, insert a long wooden skewer or cake dowel into the centre to keep the layers aligned and stabilize the cake stack. Dollop some cream on top of the cake to finish. This cake will keep, refrigerated, in an airtight container for up to 4 days. Leave it to sit at room temperature for 30 minutes before serving.

Most people who know me are aware of the fact that mango is one of my all-time favourite fruits. I can happily eat anything made with mango and here is a celebration cake packed full of it. I prefer Alphonso mango purée because it has an amazing fragrant flavour, but if you can't get hold of that specific variety, make your own purée with the mangoes available to you.

Mango mousse cake

Serves 12–14

4 large eggs

140g (5oz) caster sugar

75g (2³/₄oz) plain flour

75g (2³/₄oz) cornflour

1 teaspoon baking powder

50g (1³/₄oz) unsalted butter, melted, plus extra for greasing

50g (1³/₄oz) Alphonso mango purée

2 Alphonso mangoes, stoned, peeled and cut into cubes, to decorate

For the filling

12g packet of leaf gelatine

350g (12oz) Alphonso mango purée

80g (2³/₄oz) caster sugar

500ml (18fl oz) double cream

1 mango, stoned, peeled and diced

Preheat the oven to 180°C (350°F), Gas Mark 4. Grease a 20cm (8in) springform cake tin and line it with nonstick baking paper.

To make the cake, whisk the eggs and sugar together with an electric whisk or a stand mixer fitted with a whisk attachment for 5–7 minutes until the mixture is pale and thick and leaves a ribbon-like trail when the whisk is lifted from the bowl. Sift the plain flour, cornflour and baking powder over the mixture and fold them in carefully with a spatula or metal spoon.

Combine the melted butter and mango purée in another bowl, pour this over the egg mixture and fold it in, ensuring that you don't lose too much air from the mixture. Pour the batter into the prepared tin and bake for 35–40 minutes or until a skewer inserted in the centre comes out clean. Leave to cool in the tin.

Meanwhile, make the mango mousse for the filling. Soak the gelatine in a bowl of cold water for 10 minutes until soft. Put half the mango purée into a saucepan and add the sugar. Heat gently, stirring occasionally, until the sugar has dissolved completely. Squeeze out the softened gelatine and add it to the warm purée. Stir until the gelatine has dissolved. Then strain the warmed purée into a bowl and mix in the remaining mango purée.

In a separate bowl, whisk the cream until it forms soft peaks. Add the mango purée to the cream and fold it in until the mixture is well combined. Leave the mango mousse to cool.

Once the cake is completely cool, remove it from the tin and, using a serrated knife, cut it horizontally into 3 equal layers. Line the cake tin in which the cake was baked with clingfilm.

Carefully place 1 cake layer into the lined tin. Pour one-third of the mango mousse over the layer and spread it out evenly. Scatter one-third of the diced fresh mango over the mousse. Place a second cake layer on top, followed by half the remaining mango mousse and half the remaining mango pieces. Repeat with the final cake layer and remaining mousse and mango pieces. Transfer to the refrigerator and leave overnight to set.

When ready to eat, remove the cake from the tin, peel off the clingfilm and serve chilled, decorated with cubed mango pieces. This cake will keep, refrigerated, in an airtight container for up to 4 days.

I like to encourage people to bake with the ingredients they love, but to use them with innovation. For this cake I use one of my favourite spices, cardamom, which has a floral, citrusy quality that combines gorgeously with pistachios and milky white chocolate. This flavour combination reminds me of sweet, spicy, milky Indian desserts. They're lovely and comforting... just like this cake.

Pistachio, cardamom and white chocolate cake

Serves 10–12

For the cake

225g (8oz) unsalted butter, softened

225g (8oz) caster sugar

4 large eggs

250g (9oz) self-raising flour

1 teaspoon baking powder

1 teaspoon cardamom seeds, crushed to a fine powder

100ml (3½fl oz) milk

50g (1¾oz) pistachio nuts, roughly chopped

50g (1¾oz) white chocolate chips

For the icing and decoration

150g (5½oz) white chocolate

150g (5½oz) unsalted butter, softened

few drops of vanilla extract

handful of pistachio nuts, finely chopped

Preheat the oven to 180°C (350°F), Gas Mark 4. Grease 2 × 20cm (8in) round cake tins and line them with nonstick baking paper.

To make the cake, cream the butter and sugar together with an electric whisk or a stand mixer fitted with a whisk attachment until light and fluffy. Add the eggs, 1 at a time, ensuring that each addition is well incorporated before adding the next. Now add the flour, baking powder, cardamom and milk. Beat for 1 minute until the mixture is light and creamy. Now fold in the pistachios and white chocolate chips with a spatula. Once mixed, fill the prepared tins equally with the batter. Bake for 30 minutes until a skewer inserted into the centre of the cakes comes out clean. Leave the cakes to cool in the tins.

Once the cakes are completely cool, make the icing. Break the white chocolate into a heatproof bowl and set it over a pan of steaming water until melted, ensuring that the base of the bowl doesn't touch the water beneath it. Leave it to cool slightly. Now cream the butter in a separate bowl and add the melted chocolate and vanilla extract. Mix well until light and creamy.

Spread half the icing on 1 cake, then align the second layer on top. Spread the remaining icing on top and sprinkle with the chopped pistachios. This cake will keep in an airtight container for up to 4 days.

Saffron

Saffron is one of the least 'spicy' spices and its special
taste really has no substitute. It has a distinctive warm
aroma and flavour with a slight sweetness.

The deep crimson threads add a striking yellow-orange colour to food – and traditionally to textiles. To use saffron, simply steep the threads in a little warm water or milk for about 20 minutes before adding them to your dish. This will help ensure that the colour and flavour are evenly distributed.

There are several technical grades of saffron but, apart from the Protected Designation of Origin (PDO) awarded to saffron from La Mancha in Spain, you will rarely see mention of this on the packaging. One point to look out for, however, is the quantity of paler yellow threads among the strands: the redder the better, in this case. Provided you keep them away from heat, cold and damp, they will never spoil.

In India, saffron is particularly associated with festivals and dishes for special occasions, such as biryani. Saffron is also used to colour and flavour Indian sweets and dairy desserts such as vermicelli pudding, *shrikhand*, *kulfi* and *kheer*. My mum makes a wonderful saffron-scented rice pudding that she learned from my grandmother.

I love the combination of saffron and green cardamom, whether cooked in a savoury rice dish or in a milky dessert. With rosewater and cream, it makes a delicate filling for profiteroles and cakes, or can be churned into ice cream. Try it with citrus flavours such as lemon and orange, or in an almond cake. Rhubarb and cauliflower are two more unexpected ingredients with which saffron works very well.

Recipes featuring saffron

Saffron meringue cake (*see* page 44)

Fennel and phirni custard tartlets
(*see* page 74)

Saffron rasgulla (*see* page 92)

Saffron brioche buns with mango
cardamom cream (*see* page 119)

I first had this cake at my friend Janina's house. I fell in love with it and asked her mum for the recipe there and then. It's a Finnish cake that uses a clever technique for creating delectable layers of sponge, cream and meringue. I have altered the recipe by adding the gorgeous flavour of saffron, plus some light soft brown sugar for a caramel hit. The result is extraordinary and looks beautiful as a table centrepiece.

Saffron meringue cake

Serves 10–12

100ml (3½fl oz) milk

2 pinches of saffron threads

125g (4½oz) unsalted butter, softened, plus extra for greasing

100g (3½oz) light soft brown sugar

4 egg yolks

150g (5½oz) plain flour

2 teaspoons baking powder

For the meringue

4 egg whites

200g (7oz) caster sugar

100g (3½oz) flaked almonds

For the cream

300ml (½ pint) double cream

2 tablespoons caster sugar

To make the cake, put the milk and saffron in a small saucepan set over a low heat and slowly heat to scalding point, then turn off the heat and leave to infuse for 15 minutes.

Preheat the oven to 180°C (350°F), Gas Mark 4. Grease a 40cm × 30cm (16in × 12in) baking tin and line it with nonstick baking paper.

Cream the butter and sugar together using an electric whisk or a stand mixer fitted with a paddle attachment until light and fluffy. Add the egg yolks and beat a bit more. Now add the flour, baking powder and the infused milk. Beat briefly, until just combined. Spoon the batter into the prepared cake tin.

To prepare the meringue, whisk the egg whites in a large, very clean bowl with an electric whisk until soft peaks form, then gradually add the sugar, whisking until the meringue is stiff and shiny.

Spoon the meringue over the batter in the tin, working gently so as not to disturb the batter. Sprinkle with the almonds and bake for 25–30 minutes or until a skewer inserted into the centre of the cake comes out clean. Leave to cool in the tin.

In a clean bowl, whisk the cream and sugar together until thick. Once the cake is cool, cut it in half down the middle. Place 1 cake layer on a serving plate and spread the cream evenly on top. Align the other layer on top and neaten the edges, then serve as soon as possible. This cake is best eaten on the day it is made.

Masala chai is probably the most popular hot drink in India. My mum makes her own masala (spice mixture) for it at home and I use her tea masala recipe for this cake. Any of the popular brands of strong tea will work – there's no need to use a special variety. The fresh cream icing is a cheeky, luxurious nod to frothed milk, but I also like this cake with just a simple dusting of icing sugar – as does my whole family.

Masala chai cake

Serves 14–16

3 tea bags

100ml (3½fl oz) boiling water

200g (7oz) unsalted butter, softened, plus extra for greasing

200g (7oz) golden caster sugar

200g (7oz) self-raising flour

1 teaspoon baking powder

1 teaspoon ground cinnamon

1 teaspoon ground cardamom

½ teaspoon ground ginger

½ teaspoon ground cloves

4 large eggs

For the icing

150ml (¼ pint) double cream

1 tablespoon caster sugar

Preheat the oven to 180°C (350°F), Gas Mark 4. Grease a 25cm (10in) round cake tin and line it with nonstick baking paper.

Soak the tea bags in the measured boiling water for 10 minutes.

Cream the butter and sugar together with an electric whisk or a stand mixer fitted with a paddle attachment until light and fluffy. In a separate bowl, combine the flour, baking powder and all the spices.

Add the eggs to the butter-sugar mixture, 1 at a time, beating well after each addition. Then add the dry ingredients and the strong tea, squeezing as much liquid as you can from the tea bags. Beat it all together for 1 minute until well combined.

Pour the batter into the prepared tin and bake for 35–40 minutes or until a skewer inserted into the centre of the cake comes out clean. Leave to cool in the tin for 10 minutes, then turn out on to a wire rack and leave to cool completely.

To make the icing, whisk the cream and sugar together in a bowl until soft peaks form when the whisk is lifted from the bowl. Spread the mixture over the cooled cake to serve. This cake will keep in an airtight container for up to 5 days. It can be stored unrefrigerated as long as it is un-iced, but once the icing is on, it should be kept refrigerated.

My parents' house in India had a lime bush in the garden. As a child I would watch the fruits growing and could not wait for them to ripen so that I could make fresh lime water. This light, refreshing loaf cake uses oranges as well as limes to make it more citrusy. The black sesame seeds add flavour and a little crunch.

Black sesame and lime cake

Serves 8–10

1 tablespoon black sesame seeds

150g (5¹/₂oz) caster sugar

150g (5¹/₂oz) unsalted butter, softened, plus extra for greasing

150g (5¹/₂oz) self-raising flour

1 teaspoon baking powder

3 large eggs

finely grated zest of 2 oranges

finely grated zest of 2 limes

1 tablespoon orange juice

For the icing and decoration

100g (3¹/₂oz) icing sugar, sifted

2 tablespoons lime juice

finely grated zest of 1 lime

black sesame seeds, for sprinkling

fine strips of lime rind, for sprinkling

Preheat the oven to 180°C (350°F), Gas Mark 4. Grease a 900g (2lb) loaf tin and line it with nonstick baking paper.

In a small pan, dry-roast the sesame seeds for 2 minutes over a medium heat. Transfer to a mortar and crush them lightly with the pestle. Set aside.

Combine the remaining cake ingredients in a large mixing bowl and mix with an electric whisk for 2 minutes until the batter is light and creamy. Add the crushed sesame seeds.

Pour the batter into the prepared tin and bake for 35–40 minutes or until a skewer inserted into the centre of the cake comes out clean. Leave the cake to cool in the tin for 10 minutes, then turn out on to a wire rack and leave to cool completely.

To make the icing, mix the icing sugar with the lime juice and zest to produce a runny paste. Spoon this mixture over the cake, then sprinkle some sesame seeds and lime rind strips on top to finish. This cake will keep in an airtight container for up to 5 days.

This is a no-bake, easy-to-make cheesecake. It has a biscuit base for crunch and sweetness, covered with cardamom-flavoured pistachio cream. But the biggest flavour hit comes from the fruity chocolate ganache that is spread on top. I find cheesecakes can be overly sweet and heavy, but a tangy ganache makes them refreshing and lively.

Pistachio cheesecake with apricot chocolate ganache

Serves 10–12

300g (10¹/₂oz) digestive biscuits

150g (5¹/₂oz) butter, melted, plus extra for greasing

100g (3¹/₂oz) pistachio nuts

500g (1lb 2oz) cream cheese

90g (3¹/₄oz) icing sugar, sifted

300ml (¹/₂ pint) double cream

1 teaspoon ground cardamom

4 fresh apricots, stoned and quartered, to decorate

For the fruity ganache

300g (10¹/₂oz) fresh apricots, stoned

150g (5¹/₂oz) mango purée

50g (1³/₄oz) caster sugar

50ml (2fl oz) water

2 teaspoons lemon juice

250g (9oz) plain dark chocolate (minimum 70 per cent cocoa solids), chopped

25g (1oz) unsalted butter, softened

To make the cheesecake, blitz the digestive biscuits to fine crumbs in a food processor. Add the melted butter and mix well.

Grease a 23cm (9in) springform cake tin and line it with nonstick baking paper. Put the biscuit crumbs in the tin and press them down firmly into the base. Refrigerate while you prepare the filling.

Blitz the pistachios in a food processor until fine but not too powdery. In a bowl, beat the cream cheese and icing sugar until smooth, then fold in the pistachio nuts.

In another bowl, whisk the cream and ground cardamom together until soft peaks form. Fold into the pistachio mixture until thoroughly combined. Spoon this mixture over the biscuit base in the tin and smooth the top. Refrigerate while you prepare a fruit purée for the ganache.

Put the apricots in a pan with the mango purée, sugar and measured water. Bring to the boil, then cook over a low heat for 10 minutes. Add the lemon juice and mix well. Leave to cool for 5 minutes. Then transfer the fruit mixture to a food processor and blend until smooth. Strain into a clean bowl. Take 300g (10½oz) of the purée, put it into a saucepan and bring to the boil.

To make the ganache, put the chopped chocolate into a bowl and pour the hot fruit purée over it. Mix until the chocolate has melted. Stir in the butter until it has also melted. Pour the ganache over the cheesecake. Then transfer the cake to the refrigerator and chill for 6 hours or overnight. Remove the cake from the tin just before serving and decorate with the apricot quarters. This cheesecake will keep, refrigerated, in an airtight container for up to 4 days.

Cardamom

Aromatic cardamom is an essential ingredient in Indian and other
West Asian cuisines. It is widely used in curries, spice mixes and
sweets. It is also used to flavour tea (masala chai) and chewed
as a digestive or breath freshener.

There are two varieties. Green cardamom has
a warm, sweet, lemony flavour with clear notes
of camphor and eucalyptus, making it ideal for
adding depth and complexity to sweet bakes. By
contrast, black cardamom, which comes from a
different genus of plants, has a strong, distinctly
smoky or earthy aroma and flavour that works well
in savoury baking. It can be overpowering, so is
not suitable for light or sweet bakes. You may come
across white cardamom, which is green cardamom
that has been sun-bleached to make it blend into
paler desserts and sauces. Much of its flavour is
lost as a consequence of the bleaching process.

Cardamom can be bought in the pod, as seeds or
ready ground. Ground seeds soon lose their flavour,
so buy them whole and grind them yourself using
a pestle and mortar or coffee grinder. Or buy the
pods and remove the seeds to grind them. This is a
bit of a fiddle, but made easier if you dry-roast the
pods first, then split them open with a pestle. The
cardamom seeds from inside can be dry-roasted
to bring out their aroma and flavour.

With its citrusy tang, green cardamom goes
well with fruits such as oranges, apples, peaches,
coconut and bananas; and nuts such as almonds
and cashews. It has a natural affinity with
chocolate and is also great with coffee.

Black cardamom works well with meat and with
pulses such as lentils and chickpeas. It is a good
partner for spices such as cinnamon and cloves. A
little cardamom goes a long way, so use it sparingly.

Recipes featuring cardamom

A project for when you really want to impress, this cake begs to be served at celebrations and has the advantage of suiting your gluten-free guests. My kids adore macarons, and when I first made this gigantic version they asked me to make it again for their birthdays. The combination of flavours is unique – rose, pistachio and sesame brittle are each very popular in India, although they are not usually used all together, and chocolate gives the whole thing a great finish.

Sesame, pistachio and rose macaron cake

Serves 10–12

For the macaron

170g (6oz) icing sugar, sifted

160g (5¾oz) ground almonds

120g (4¼oz) egg whites (from about 3 eggs)

few drops of pink food colouring

½ teaspoon rosewater

160g (5¾oz) caster sugar

50ml (2fl oz) water

For the pistachio custard

30g (1oz) pistachio nuts

1 teaspoon toasted sesame oil

250ml (9fl oz) milk

60g (2¼oz) egg yolks (about 3 yolks)

50g (1¾oz) caster sugar

25g (1oz) plain flour

200g (7oz) unsalted butter, softened

Line 2 baking trays with nonstick baking paper and draw a 20cm (8in) circle on each tray.

To make the macaron, put the icing sugar and almonds in a bowl. Add 60g (2¼oz) of the egg whites and mix well. Add the pink food colouring and rosewater and mix again.

In a saucepan, gently heat the caster sugar and measured water until the sugar has completely dissolved, then bring to a simmer. Put a sugar thermometer in the pan and heat to 115°C (239°F). Once the syrup has reached 110°C (230°F), start whisking the remaining egg whites in a stand mixer. Whisk on a high speed until they form stiff peaks, by which time the syrup will have reached the correct temperature, then slowly pour the sugar syrup into the whisked egg whites while whisking continuously. Keep whisking on a high speed until the meringue has cooled down in the bowl.

Fold the almond mixture thoroughly into the meringue. Spoon the mixture into a piping bag fitted with a 12mm (½in) round piping nozzle and pipe it in 3 large discs over the guides you drew on the baking paper. Leave to rest for 30–40 minutes or until the top of the discs are dry.

Preheat the oven to 160°C (325°F), Gas Mark 3. Bake the macaron discs for 25–30 minutes until they are dry on the outsides.

To make the custard, grind the pistachios with the sesame oil until very fine using a spice grinder, food processor or a pestle and mortar. In a small pan, slowly heat the milk to scalding point. In a bowl, whisk the egg yolks and sugar together with an electric whisk until pale and creamy. Add the flour and whisk well. Slowly add the hot milk, whisking continuously. Pour the custard back into the saucepan and cook over a low heat for 6–8 minutes, stirring, until thick. Pour the custard into the bowl of a stand mixer and beat it until it reaches room temperature. Gradually add the butter, a little at a time, beating until it is fully incorporated, then add the pistachio paste and mix well. When you are sure that the mixture has cooled completely, spoon it into a piping bag fitted with a 12mm (½in) round nozzle and set aside.

For the sesame brittle and chocolate ganache

oil, for greasing

120g (4¼oz) caster sugar

2 tablespoons water

50g (1¾oz) sesame seeds

300ml (½ pint) double cream

150g (5½oz) plain dark chocolate (minimum 70 per cent cocoa solids)

100g (3½oz) milk chocolate

25g (1oz) unsalted butter, softened

To make the sesame brittle, lightly oil a sheet of nonstick baking paper. Heat the sugar and measured water in a pan set over a low heat until they form a caramel. Remove from the heat, quickly mix in the sesame seeds, then pour the caramel on to the oiled baking paper. Leave to cool completely and, once cool, grind three-quarters of the brittle to a coarse powder using the spice grinder, food processor or pestle and mortar. Set aside the remaining brittle to use as decoration.

To make the ganache, slowly heat the cream to scalding point in a pan. Break and combine both the chocolates in a heatproof bowl, then slowly pour in the hot cream. Mix well until the chocolate has melted. Add the butter and mix until it has also melted. Stir in 6 tablespoons of the finely ground sesame brittle. Refrigerate for 1 hour or until slightly set, then spoon the ganache into a piping bag fitted with a 12mm (½in) round nozzle and set aside.

To assemble, place 1 of the rose macaron discs upside down on a serving plate. Pipe little balls of chocolate ganache around the edge of the macaron, then pipe a spiral of ganache in the centre to cover the whole disc, using about half of the ganache. Place the second macaron disc on top and pipe little balls of pistachio custard over it. Place the third macaron disc on top, then pipe balls of the remaining ganache onto the centre of the disc. Decorate with a few broken pieces of the remaining sesame brittle and serve. This macaron cake is best eaten the day it is made.

Although I do a lot of gluten-free cooking, I tend not to make many gluten-free cakes. I devised this recipe for a friend who is coeliac, and it turned out so well that my kids often ask for this chocolate mousse cake. It has a lovely hint of sweet star anise, which goes well with chocolate, and a lemon syrup balances the richness. It's not a common flavour combination, but it works.

Star anise and lemon chocolate mousse cake

Serves 10–12

5 large eggs

250g (9oz) caster sugar

125ml (4fl oz) water

finely grated zest of 1 lemon

1 teaspoon ground star anise

300g (10½oz) plain dark chocolate (minimum 70 per cent cocoa solids), roughly chopped

50g (1¾oz) milk chocolate, roughly chopped

225g (8oz) unsalted butter, diced, plus extra for greasing

For the syrup

175g (6oz) natural cane sugar

5 tablespoons water

2 lemons (unpeeled), thinly sliced

Preheat the oven to 160°C (325°F), Gas Mark 3. Grease a 23cm (9in) round cake tin and line it with nonstick baking paper.

To make the mousse cake, whisk the eggs with 150g (5½oz) of the caster sugar using an electric whisk or a stand mixer fitted with a whisk attachment for 5–7 minutes until the mixture is pale and doubled in size. It should leave a ribbon-like trail when the whisk is lifted from the bowl.

Heat the remaining caster sugar with the measured water in a saucepan set over a low heat until the sugar has melted. Add the lemon zest and ground star anise and mix well. Next, add both chocolates and the butter and stir until they have melted. Fold this into the egg mixture, ensuring that the batter doesn't lose too much air. Spoon the batter into the prepared tin and place the tin in a large roasting tin.

Transfer to the oven and carefully pour boiling water into the roasting tin so that it reaches halfway up the side of the cake tin. Bake for 50–55 minutes until a crispy skin has formed on the cake's surface and a skewer inserted into the centre of the cake comes out with a little cake mix still on it. Set aside until warm.

To make the syrup, heat the cane sugar and measured water in a saucepan set over a low heat until the sugar has melted. Add the lemon slices and cook over a low heat for 15–20 minutes.

With the warm cake still in its tin, gently spoon the syrup over it. Arrange the lemon slices on top. Leave to set at room temperature for a while, then transfer it to a serving plate. You can enjoy the cake very gooey or, if you prefer it to be more set, chill it for a couple of hours before serving. This cake will keep, refrigerated, in an airtight container for up to 3 days.

When I was a child, my dad would bring home bunches of fresh lychees whenever they were in season. I remember enjoying the juicy sweet fruits with my sisters, and since then I have always loved lychees. This very moist cake features a little caramel to enhance the flavour of the fruit. You will have some leftover sauce, which will keep, refrigerated, for up to two weeks. Finish it up with bowls of ice cream and other desserts.

Lychee cake

Serves 10–12

400g (14oz) canned lychees

200g (7oz) unsalted butter, softened, plus extra for greasing

150g (5½oz) caster sugar, plus 4 tablespoons

4 large eggs

150g (5½oz) self-raising flour

50g (1¾oz) ground almonds

1 teaspoon baking powder

For the caramel sauce

100g (3½oz) caster sugar

2 tablespoons water

40g (1½oz) unsalted butter, diced

4 tablespoons double cream

For the decoration

300ml (½ pint) double cream

200g (7oz) canned lychees (drained weight) or fresh peeled and pitted lychees, halved

Preheat the oven to 180°C (350°F), Gas Mark 4. Grease 2 × 20cm (8in) cake tins and line them with nonstick baking paper.

To make the cake, drain the canned lychees, reserving the syrup, then chop the fruit into small pieces and set aside.

Cream the butter and the 150g (5½oz) sugar together with an electric whisk or a stand mixer fitted with a paddle attachment until light and fluffy. Add the eggs, 1 at a time, beating well after each addition. Add the dry ingredients and beat for 1 minute until thoroughly combined.

Fold the chopped lychees into the cake batter, then pour the mixture equally into the prepared tins. Bake for 25–30 minutes or until a skewer inserted into the centres of the cakes comes out clean. Leave the cakes to cool in the tins for 10 minutes, then turn out on to a wire rack and leave to cool completely.

Meanwhile, in a small saucepan, combine the reserved syrup from the lychees and add the remaining 4 tablespoons caster sugar. Bring to the boil, then simmer until the volume of the liquid has reduced by half. Remove from the heat and leave to cool.

When both the cakes and syrup are cool, brush the syrup over the cakes.

To make the caramel sauce, combine the caster sugar and measured water in a small saucepan and cook for 5–6 minutes until the mixture turns into a golden-brown caramel. Stir in the butter and cook for another couple of minutes. Now slowly add the cream, stirring continuously. Cook for a further 2 minutes, then set aside to cool.

To prepare the decoration, whisk the double cream in a bowl until soft peaks form. Add 2–3 tablespoons of the cooled caramel sauce and fold it in. To assemble, place the cake on a serving plate and spread half the flavoured cream on it. Sit the second cake over the cream and spread the remainder of the flavoured cream on top. Decorate with the lychees and drizzle with some of the remaining caramel sauce. This cake will keep, refrigerated, in an airtight container for up to 4 days. Let it sit at room temperature for 30 minutes before serving.

This very light sponge is my mother's most-requested cake; she has been making it for years and her friends and relatives love it. It makes the perfect end to a meal. I top it with a very delicious sauce that is sweet and rich, in the manner of sticky toffee pudding. Do skip the sauce if you prefer, because the cake is heavenly on its own or with just a sprinkling of icing sugar.

Date, walnut and nutmeg cake

Serves 14–16

130g (4½oz) pitted dates, roughly chopped

200ml (⅓ pint) water

150g (5½oz) unsalted butter, softened, plus extra for greasing

150g (5½oz) light muscovado sugar

3 eggs

1 teaspoon bicarbonate of soda

300g (10½oz) self-raising flour

50g (1¾oz) walnuts, roughly chopped

½ teaspoon ground nutmeg

vanilla ice cream, to serve (optional)

For the sauce (optional)

50g (1¾oz) unsalted butter

90g (3¼oz) dark muscovado sugar

350ml (12fl oz) double cream

5 tablespoons golden syrup

100g (3½oz) walnuts, roughly chopped

Preheat the oven to 180°C (350°F), Gas Mark 4. Grease a bundt tin of your choice; I like a plain ring tin, which makes this cake look beautifully simple.

In a saucepan, bring the dates and measured water to the boil, then reduce the heat to low and cook for 10 minutes. Set aside to cool.

Cream the butter and sugar together using an electric whisk or a stand mixer fitted with a paddle attachment until light and fluffy. Add the eggs, 1 at a time, beating well after each addition. Add the bicarbonate of soda and flour and beat well again. Fold in the cooled cooked dates with any remaining cooking water, along with the walnuts and nutmeg.

Spoon the batter into the prepared tin and bake for 30–35 minutes until a skewer inserted into the centre of the cake comes out clean. Leave the cake to cool in the tin for 5 minutes while you prepare the sauce, if using.

In a saucepan, combine the butter, sugar, cream and golden syrup and bring to the boil. Simmer for 5 minutes over a low heat. Stir in the walnuts, then take the pan off the heat.

Remove the cake from the tin and position it on a serving plate. Pour the hot sauce over the cake and leave it to soak in. Serve with vanilla ice cream, if liked. This cake will keep in an airtight container for up to 4 days. You can warm it in a microwave oven for few seconds before serving, if liked.

Pies and tarts

I love fresh peaches and even planted a peach tree in my garden in England. Sadly, it did not survive, but my love for the fruit has. Here I am using star anise to give a liquorice flavour to the peaches, which nestle in a frangipane-style filling.

Peach, star anise and almond tart

Serves 10–12

For the pastry

200g (7oz) plain flour, plus extra for dusting

20g (³/₄oz) golden caster sugar

100g (3¹/₂oz) chilled unsalted butter, diced

1 large egg

1 teaspoon lemon juice

For the filling

2 fresh peaches

100g (3¹/₂oz) unsalted butter, softened

100g (3¹/₂oz) caster sugar

50g (1³/₄oz) ground almonds

100g (3¹/₂oz) plain flour

finely grated zest of 1 orange

2 large eggs

1 teaspoon ground star anise

20g (³/₄oz) flaked almonds

icing sugar, for dusting

To make the pastry, mix the flour and sugar in a large bowl. Add the diced butter and coat it in the flour. Using your fingertips, rub the butter into the flour until the mixture resembles breadcrumbs.

Mix the egg and lemon juice together, then pour into the flour mixture just enough of this liquid to bring the dough together – you might not need all the liquid. Gently knead the dough on a lightly floured surface for a few seconds, then shape it into a ball. Wrap the dough in clingfilm and leave to rest in the refrigerator for 10–15 minutes.

Preheat the oven to 180°C (350°F), Gas Mark 4. On a floured surface, roll out the dough to the thickness of 3mm (⅛in). Line a 23cm (9in) loose-bottomed tart tin with the dough, leaving the excess dough overhanging the edge of the tin. Prick the base all over with a fork.

Line the pastry case with nonstick baking paper, fill it with baking beans and bake for 15 minutes. Remove the paper and beans and bake for a further 20 minutes or until the pastry looks dry and crisp. Use a small sharp knife to trim away the excess pastry from the rim, then leave the tart case to cool in the tin for 15 minutes.

Meanwhile, make the filling. Pop the peaches in a pan of boiling water for 1 minute, then remove them and plunge them immediately into cold water for 1 minute. Gently peel off the skins, then remove the stones and cut the fruit into thin slices.

In a bowl, combine the butter, caster sugar, ground almonds, flour, orange zest, eggs and star anise and whisk with an electric whisk for 2 minutes until the mixture is pale and light. Pour the mixture into the pastry case and arrange the sliced peaches on top. Sprinkle the flaked almonds over and bake for 35–40 minutes until light golden and cooked through. Leave the tart to cool in the tin for 10 minutes, then transfer to a serving plate, dust with icing sugar and serve. This tart will keep in an airtight container for up to 3 days.

I love tarte au citron and here is my take on this classic dish. Fresh passion fruit gives it a lovely sourness that is very refreshing and perfect for summer. Sometimes I top this tart with meringue and bake it for further a 10–15 minutes to make it extra special.

Passion fruit, lime and ginger tart

Serves 10–12

For the pastry

200g (7oz) plain flour, plus extra for dusting

20g (³/₄oz) golden caster sugar

100g (3¹/₂oz) chilled unsalted butter, diced

1 large egg

1 teaspoon lemon juice

For the filling

5 large eggs

200g (7oz) caster sugar

135ml (4¹/₂fl oz) double cream

1 teaspoon ground ginger

finely grated zest and juice of 4 limes

pulp of 4 passion fruit, sieved

icing sugar, for dusting

To make the pastry, mix the flour and sugar together in a large bowl. Add the diced butter and coat it in the flour. Using your fingertips, rub the butter into the flour until the mixture resembles breadcrumbs.

Mix the egg and lemon juice together, then pour into the flour mixture just enough of this liquid to bring the dough together – you might not need all the liquid. Gently knead the dough on a lightly floured surface for a few seconds, then shape it into a ball. Wrap it in clingfilm and leave to rest in the refrigerator for 10–15 minutes.

Preheat the oven to 180°C (350°F), Gas Mark 4. On a floured surface, roll out the dough to a thickness of 3mm (¹/₈in). Line a 23cm (9in) loose-bottomed tart tin with the dough, leaving the excess dough overhanging the edge of the tin. Prick the base all over with a fork.

Line the pastry case with nonstick baking paper, fill it with baking beans and bake for 15 minutes. Remove the paper and beans and bake for a further 20 minutes or until the pastry looks dry and crisp. Use a small sharp knife to trim away the excess pastry from the rim, then leave the tart case to cool in the tin for 15 minutes.

To make the filling, in a large bowl, whisk the eggs and sugar together with an electric whisk for 3–4 minutes or until creamy and fluffy. Add the cream, ground ginger, lime zest and juice and passion fruit pulp and mix well. Pour the filling into the cooled pastry case and bake for 30–35 minutes or until the filling is just set and has a slight wobble in the centre. Leave the tart to cool in the tin slightly, then transfer to a serving plate. Dust with icing sugar and serve.

Mango, one of my favourite fruits, is also one of the most popular summer fruits in India. It comes in many varieties, of which Alphonso is probably the best known in the UK. I love the depth of flavour and colour you have with a mango, and in this tart it comes in the form of a creamy filling that contrasts beautifully with a very crunchy chocolate pastry case. Everyone loves a bit of chocolate in their baking, after all! Use any medium-sized fresh ripe mango or, because it is being processed into a pulp, substitute ready-made mango purée.

Chocolate and mango tart

Serves 10–12

For the chocolate pastry

2 egg yolks

¼ teaspoon vanilla extract

100g (3½oz) golden caster sugar

100g (3½oz) unsalted butter, softened

165g (5¾oz) plain flour

30g (1oz) cocoa powder

pinch of salt

For the mango filling and decoration

5 large eggs

175g (6oz) golden caster sugar

125ml (4fl oz) double cream

finely grated zest of 2 lemons

1 mango, stoned, peeled and puréed, then sieved (to yield roughly 150g/5½oz purée)

2 mangoes, stoned, peeled and sliced

Preheat the oven to 180°C (350°F), Gas Mark 4.

To make the pastry, mix the egg yolks, vanilla extract and sugar together in a bowl. To this, add the butter and mix briefly. Now add the flour, cocoa powder and salt and, with minimum handling, bring the dough together. Now knead it for a couple of seconds, shape it into a ball and wrap it in clingfilm. Chill for 30 minutes.

Roll out the dough to a thickness of roughly 3mm (⅛in). (For a thin and evenly rolled expanse of dough, try rolling it between 2 sheets of clingfilm.) Place a 23cm (9in) tart tin on a baking tray and line it with the dough, allowing the excess to overhang the edge of the tin. Chill for 15 minutes.

Place a large piece of nonstick baking paper in the pastry-lined tin, fill the case with baking beans and bake for 20 minutes. Remove the paper and beans and bake for another 10 minutes or until firm and crispy – because this is a chocolate pastry, you need to keep a close eye on it to avoid burning. Leave to cool in the tin for 15 minutes, then cut away the excess pastry with a sharp knife.

To make the mango filling, whisk the eggs in a bowl until well combined. Now add the sugar, cream, lemon zest and mango purée and mix well. Transfer the filling to a jug and pour it into the cool pastry case. Bake for 25–30 minutes or until the filling is just set with a slight wobble in the centre.

Leave to cool in the tin until the filling seems set enough, and then remove from the tin and transfer to a serving plate. Decorate the tart with the slices of mango. This tart will keep, refrigerated, in an airtight container for up to 4 days.

There is an absolutely delicious Indian dessert called *dal ka halwa*, which uses yellow split lentils, sugar and ghee. It tends to be made on special occasions and is very popular for wedding feasts. I use that halwa as a filling for this filo pastry pie. The fine, crispy pastry goes extraordinarily well with the rich, sweet filling. Serve it hot or cold with fresh cream or ice cream.

Halwa tart

Serves 10–12

5 sheets of filo pastry

75g (2³/₄oz) butter, melted, plus extra for greasing

For the filling

150g (5¹/₂oz) yellow split lentils (*moong dal*)

400ml (14fl oz) water

75g (2³/₄oz) ghee

140g (5oz) icing sugar, sifted

1 teaspoon ground cardamom

50ml (2fl oz) milk

50g (1³/₄oz) blanched almonds, roughly chopped

Preheat the oven to 180°C (350°F), Gas Mark 4. Grease a 20cm (8in) tart tin.

For the filling, soak the lentils in 250ml (9fl oz) of the measured water for 1 hour. Grind them with the soaking water to a coarse paste in a food processor.

Heat the ghee in a shallow pan, add the lentil paste and mix well. Cook over a medium–low heat for 30–35 minutes, stirring every 5 minutes, until the mixture turns a deep golden brown. It will become very gluey and stick to the pan, but don't let this stop you – continue cooking and it will become oily. When the mixture no longer sticks to the pan, it is perfectly cooked.

Stir in the remaining measured water, along with the icing sugar, ground cardamom and milk and cook over a low heat for 5 minutes until everything is amalgamated. Add the almonds, stir well, then take the pan off the heat and leave to cool for 10–15 minutes.

Carefully unroll the filo pastry sheets and cover them with a clean, damp tea towel to prevent them drying out. Lay 1 sheet of pastry in the prepared tart tin and brush with some of the melted butter. Allow the excess pastry to overhang the sides of the tin. Lay another pastry sheet on top and brush with more butter. Continue in this way until you have used all 5 sheets. Spoon the filling into the pastry case, then fold the layers of overhanging pastry into the middle to cover the filling, brushing each layer with melted butter.

Sit the tart tin on a baking tray and bake for 25–30 minutes until the pastry is crisp and golden brown. Leave to cool in the tin for 10 minutes, then transfer to a serving plate. This tart is best eaten the same day, as the filo pastry will become soft. The halwa filling will keep, refrigerated, in an airtight container for up to 6 days.

Phirni is a type of Indian rice pudding that is left to set and then served in small clay pots. Here, I enrich it with eggs and replace the clay pots with crisp pastry to give a crunchy finish. Fennel seeds add an amazing flavour when combined with the traditional saffron. Serve these little tarts just as they are, or top them with any combination of fruits and nuts that suits you.

Fennel and phirni custard tartlets

Makes 6

For the pastry

200g (7oz) plain flour

25g (1oz) ground almonds

40g (1½oz) icing sugar, sifted

pinch of salt

¼ teaspoon vanilla bean paste

125g (4½oz) chilled unsalted butter, diced, plus extra for greasing

1 large egg yolk

about 1 teaspoon cold water

For the *phirni* custard

100g (3½oz) white basmati or other long-grain rice

400ml (14fl oz) boiling water

850ml (1½ pints) milk

2 tablespoons fennel seeds, toasted and roughly crushed

125g (4½oz) granulated sugar

2 pinches of saffron threads

1 large egg, plus 1 large egg yolk, beaten together

For the decoration (optional)

fruits

nuts

ice cream

To make the pastry, mix the flour, almonds, icing sugar, salt and vanilla together in a large bowl. Add the butter cubes and rub them into the flour with your fingertips until the mixture resembles breadcrumbs. Add the egg yolk and bring the dough together. If the dough is a bit dry, add the measured water. Knead the dough for a few seconds, then shape it into a cylinder. Wrap this in clingfilm and chill for 15 minutes.

Grease 6 tartlet tins. Slice the roll of dough into 6 equal pieces. Roll out 1 piece of dough into a circle with a thickness of 2mm (¹/₁₆in). Line 1 of the prepared tins with this dough circle, allowing the excess dough to overhang the edge of the tin. Repeat with the remaining pieces of dough. Place the tins on a baking tray and chill for 15 minutes.

Preheat the oven to 180°C (350°F), Gas Mark 4. Cut 6 squares of nonstick baking paper and put them in the pastry-lined tins. Fill the cases with baking beans. Bake for 15 minutes, then remove the baking beans and paper and bake for a further 10–15 minutes until golden and crisp. Leave to cool in the tins for 10 minutes, then cut away the excess pastry with a sharp knife. Leave the tart cases in the tins to cool completely.

To make the *phirni* custard, put the rice in a bowl, cover with the measured boiling water and leave to soak for 30 minutes. Now grind the mixture to a thick, coarse paste in a food processor. Put the milk in a saucepan with the crushed fennel seeds and slowly bring to the boil. Add the coarse rice paste and cook over a low heat for 15 minutes, stirring frequently. Add the sugar and saffron and mix well. Gradually add the beaten eggs, stirring continuously. Cook for a further 5 minutes until the custard is thick.

Pour the *phirni* custard into a clean bowl and cover the surface with clingfilm to prevent a skin forming. Refrigerate the custard to chill.

When ready to serve, spoon the custard into a disposable piping bag, cut off the tip and pipe it into the cooled tart cases. Finish with fruits, nuts and ice cream, as preferred. Remove the tartlets from the tins to serve. The tart cases will keep for up to 3 days in an airtight container. The custard will keep, refrigerated, for up to 3 days in an airtight container. Assemble just before serving.

Fennel

My mother doesn't use fennel a lot in cooking, yet she always
has a small jar of dry-roasted fennel seeds next to the dining table.
These are nibbled after meals to help with digestion, not just in
her home but in many throughout India. Fennel is also a popular
mouth freshener, whether the seeds are sold sugar-coated,
bathed in syrup or included in *paan*, the mix of areca nut, herbs,
spices and often tobacco, wrapped in betel leaves and
sold on street-side stalls.

Fennel seeds are plump green or greeny brown, with a sweet, warm aroma and a mild flavour of aniseed. They are famously paired with fish and seafood in many cuisines, as they cut the richness of oily fish species, and heighten and freshen the sweetness of shellfish. However, fennel also goes well with meats, elegantly counteracting their fattiness. In French cooking, you will often find fennel used in cream sauces, sometimes with aniseed-flavoured spirits such as pastis underlining the fennel's herbal tang.

In Indian cuisine, fennel is essential to the East Indian spice mix *panch phoran* (literally, 'five spices'), in which it combines with cumin, nigella (*kalonji*), fenugreek and black mustard seeds to flavour a wide range of dishes, including chicken curries, fish, lentils, vegetables and pickles. One of the important things about *panch phoran* is that the seeds are all used whole rather than ground, and usually fried together in oil at the beginning of a dish.

Fennel is also very popular in Gujarati snacks and in Kashmiri dishes including paneer masala, rogan josh and *dum aloo* (potatoes in spicy gravy).

It is best to buy fennel seeds and toast and grind them as required. When experimenting in the kitchen, try adding toasted crushed seeds to salad dressings and mayonnaise.

Toasted whole, seeds give a lovely flavour to bread doughs. Fennel is also good in sweet bakes. Try some toasted crushed seeds in whipped cream when icing cakes, or add them along with saffron to custard mixtures – the combination is very refreshing. Fennel also goes well with fruits, including oranges, apples and pears, and add interest to tatin-style fruit tarts. Almonds and walnuts are other good partners, so try adding some to nut brittles and pralines, too.

Recipes featuring fennel

India has many varieties of red chillies. This curried chicken pie features *degi mirch*, a time-honoured crimson chilli powder blend with a mild yet distinctive flavour. This is perfect comfort food.

Degi mirch chicken pie

Serves 6–8

For the chicken curry filling

4 tablespoons vegetable oil

2 black cardamom pods

4 green cardamom pods

4 cloves

2.5cm (1in) cinnamon stick

4 onions, thinly sliced

5 garlic cloves, finely chopped

2.5cm (1in) piece of fresh root ginger, peeled and finely chopped

1kg (2lb 4oz) boneless, skinless chicken breast, cut into 2.5cm (1in) cubes

2 teaspoons *degi mirch*

150ml (¼ pint) natural yogurt

1 teaspoon ground cumin

2 teaspoons ground coriander

1 teaspoon garam masala

½ teaspoon ground turmeric

2 teaspoons salt

100ml (3½fl oz) boiling water

For the pastry

300g (10½oz) plain flour, plus extra for dusting

pinch of salt

½ teaspoon ground turmeric

150g (5½oz) chilled unsalted butter, diced

2 teaspoons dried fenugreek leaves (*kasuri methi*)

4–6 tablespoons cold water

1 egg, beaten

First make the curry filling. Heat the oil in a large pan over a medium heat and add all the cardamom pods, cloves and cinnamon. Cook for about 1 minute until they start to change colour, then add the onions. Cook until they become golden brown, then add the garlic and ginger and cook for 2 minutes more.

Add the chicken pieces, increase the heat to high and cook for 5 minutes, stirring often. Add the *degi mirch* and mix well.

In a small bowl, combine the yogurt, cumin, coriander, garam masala, turmeric and salt. Mix this into the chicken, then pour in the measured boiling water. Cover with a lid and simmer for 15–20 minutes or until the chicken is cooked. Set aside to cool.

Preheat the oven to 200°C (400°F), Gas Mark 6.

To make the pastry, combine the flour, salt and turmeric in a mixing bowl. Add the butter and rub it into the flour with your fingertips until the mixture resembles breadcrumbs. Stir in the *kasuri methi*, then add the measured water, a little at a time, and bring the dough together. Gently knead it on a work surface for 1 minute, then shape it into a ball. Wrap this in clingfilm and chill for 10 minutes.

Tip the chicken curry filling into a 23cm (9in) pie dish. On a lightly floured surface, roll out the dough to a thickness of 3mm (⅛in). From this sheet of dough, cut a long strip that is 1cm (½in) wide. Dampen the rim of the pie dish with water, then press down the dough strip along the rim. Dampen this, too.

Cover the pie with the remaining dough sheet and press down around the edge to seal. Trim off the excess dough. Press a design into the lid using a fork or make a pattern with your fingertips, then pinch the edge to seal. Cut a cross in the centre of the pie to let out the steam. If you like, decorate the top of the pie with leaves or other designs cut from the dough trimmings. Brush the top of the pie with beaten egg, then bake for 30–35 minutes until crisp and golden. The pie will keep, refrigerated, for up to 3 days in an airtight container. Heat it in an oven preheated to 180°C (350°F), Gas Mark 4 for 10–15 minutes before serving.

I love the look of traditional English hand-raised pies and wanted to create a meat-free version. This dal filling has an appealing, fresh look and is packed with flavour, including a tangy sourness from the *amchur* (mango powder). The pie makes a great main course served with Indian Coleslaw (*see* page 232) or a Sunday lunch served with roast potatoes and Onion Chutney (*see* page 227).

Moong dal pie

Serves 8–10

For the filling

300g (10½oz) green lentils (*sabut moong dal*)

100g (3½oz) yellow lentils (*chana dal*)

1½ teaspoons salt

1 litre (1¾ pints) water

2 tablespoons vegetable oil

1 teaspoon cumin seeds

10 curry leaves

3 tomatoes, roughly chopped

2.5cm (1in) piece of fresh root ginger, peeled and grated

1 teaspoon garam masala

1 teaspoon mango powder (*amchur*)

½ teaspoon chilli powder

For the pastry

450g (1lb) plain flour

100g (3½oz) strong white bread flour

75g (2¾oz) chilled unsalted butter, diced, plus extra for greasing

200ml (⅓ pint) water

½ teaspoon salt

100g (3½oz) vegetable or lard shortening

1 egg yolk, beaten

To make the filling, put the green and yellow lentils in a large saucepan with the salt and measured water. Bring to the boil, half-cover with a lid and simmer over a low heat for 30–35 minutes or until the lentils are cooked and have absorbed the water.

In a separate pan, heat the oil over a medium heat. Add the cumin seeds and curry leaves and stir for a few seconds, then add the tomatoes and ginger and cook for 2 minutes more. Add the cooked lentils, garam masala, mango powder and chilli powder. Mix well and cook for 2 minutes. Then take the pan off the heat and set aside.

Now make the crust. Preheat the oven to 200°C (400°F), Gas Mark 6. Grease a 20cm (8in) round cake tin that is 8cm (3¼in) deep.

Combine the flours in a mixing bowl, add the butter and rub it in with your fingertips until the mixture resembles breadcrumbs.

In a saucepan, heat the measured water, salt and shortening or lard until just simmering. Carefully pour this mixture on to the flour mixture and mix it all together with a wooden spoon. Once the mixture is cool enough to handle, bring the dough together and knead it for a few seconds on a clean work surface. Set aside about one-third of the dough to make the lid. Roll the rest into a circle that is large enough to line the tin. Ease the circle into the tin with the excess dough overhanging the edge, ensuring that there are no cracks or holes in the dough.

Spoon the lentil filling into the pastry case. Roll the reserved dough into a circle to make the pie lid. Brush the rim of the pastry case with beaten egg yolk and lay the lid on top. Press the edges together to seal. Trim off the excess dough to neaten, then crimp the edge to give a nice pattern. Cut a cross in the centre of the lid to allow steam to escape. Brush the pie lid with beaten egg yolk, then bake for 1 hour.

Leave the pie to cool in the tin for 15 minutes, then transfer it to a serving plate. Serve warm or cold. This pie will keep, refrigerated, in an airtight container for up to 3 days. Warm it in an oven preheated to 180°C (350°F), Gas Mark 4 before serving.

My twist on quiche, this tasty tart is filled with onions cooked the South Indian way, with fresh curry leaves, mustard seeds and red chillies. They work a treat with this smoked paprika pastry, which has an attractive reddish hue. Serve slices of this tart with a spoonful of Coconut Chutney (*see* page 226).

Curry onion tart

Serves 10–12

For the pastry

300g (10½oz) plain flour, plus extra for dusting

pinch of salt

1 tablespoon smoked paprika

150g (5½oz) chilled salted butter, diced

1 teaspoon lemon juice

4–6 tablespoons cold water

For the filling

2 tablespoons vegetable oil

2 teaspoons black mustard seeds

10–15 curry leaves

4 dried red chillies

4 onions, thinly sliced

handful of fresh coriander leaves, finely chopped

1 teaspoon salt

2 large eggs

1 egg yolk

100ml (3½fl oz) double cream

To make the pastry, mix the flour, salt and paprika together in a large bowl. Add the butter and coat it with the flour. Use your fingertips to rub the butter into the flour until the mixture resembles breadcrumbs. Mix the lemon juice and measured water together and pour in just enough of the liquid to bring the dough together. Gently knead the dough on a lightly floured surface for a few seconds, then shape it into a ball. Wrap the ball in clingfilm and chill for 10–15 minutes.

Preheat the oven to 180°C (350°F), Gas Mark 4. On a floured work surface, roll out the dough to a thickness of 3mm (⅛in). Line a 23cm (9in) loose-bottomed tart tin with the dough, leaving the excess dough overhanging the edge. Prick the dough all over with a fork, then line it with nonstick baking paper, fill it with baking beans and bake for 15 minutes. Remove the paper and beans and bake for a further 20 minutes or until the pastry looks dry and crisp. Use a small, sharp knife to trim away the excess pastry from the rim, then leave the tart case to cool in the tin for 15 minutes.

While the tart case is cooking, prepare the filling. Heat the oil in a pan over a medium heat and add the mustard seeds, curry leaves and dried chillies. When the mustard seeds start to pop, add the onions and cook over a medium heat until light golden. Stir in the coriander and salt, take the pan off the heat and leave to cool for a few minutes.

Whisk the whole eggs, yolk and cream together in a bowl. Fill the baked tart case with the onions and press them down a little. Sit the tart tin on a baking tray, then pour the egg mixture over the onions. Bake for 35 minutes or until the filling is set and golden. Leave the tart to cool in the tin for 10 minutes, then transfer it to a serving plate. Enjoy it warm or cold. This tart will keep in an airtight container for up to 2 days, or refrigerated for up to 4 days.

Serve this delicious *chana*-filled pie in winter with roast potatoes and vegetables, or in summer with salads, chutney and raita.

Chickpea curry pie

Serves 8–10

For the chickpea curry

2 tablespoons vegetable oil

1 teaspoon cumin seeds

2 bay leaves

1 cinnamon stick

3 black cardamom pods

2 green cardamom pods

3 onions, finely chopped

3 garlic cloves, finely grated

2.5cm (1in) piece of fresh root ginger, peeled and grated

3 tomatoes, finely chopped

1¹/₂ teaspoons salt

¹/₂ teaspoon chilli powder

¹/₂ teaspoon ground turmeric

2 teaspoons ground coriander

1 teaspoon garam masala

1 teaspoon ground cumin

2 x 400g (14oz) cans chickpeas

handful of fresh coriander leaves, finely chopped

For the pastry

450g (1lb) plain flour, plus extra for dusting

100g (3¹/₂oz) strong white bread flour

1 tablespoon *degi mirch*

75g (2³/₄oz) unsalted butter, diced, plus extra for greasing

200ml (¹/₃ pint) water

100g (3¹/₂oz) vegetable shortening or lard

¹/₂ teaspoon salt

1 egg, beaten

To make the curry, heat the oil in a pan over a medium heat. Add the cumin seeds, bay leaves, cinnamon and the black and green cardamom pods and cook for 1 minute until everything starts to change colour. Add the onions and cook over a low heat until they are dark golden – reaching this stage with the onions is vital to getting the flavour of the curry right.

Add the grated garlic and ginger and cook for 2 minutes, then add the tomatoes. Cook, stirring occasionally, for 10–15 minutes until the tomatoes are well incorporated.

Mix in the salt, chilli powder, turmeric, ground coriander, garam masala and ground cumin and cook for 2 minutes. Tip the chickpeas and all their liquid into the pan. Cook over a low heat for 10–15 minutes. Mash a few chickpeas lightly to thicken the gravy, then stir in the chopped coriander. Cover the saucepan with a lid, take it off the heat and set aside to cool.

Preheat the oven to 200°C (400°F), Gas Mark 6. Grease a 20cm (8in) springform cake tin that is 7–8cm (2³/₄–3¹/₄in) deep.

To make the pastry, combine the flours, *desi mirch* and butter and rub the butter in with your fingertips until the mixture resembles breadcrumbs. In a saucepan, heat the measured water, shortening or lard and salt until the fat has melted and the liquid is just simmering. Pour this liquid into the flour mixture and stir with a wooden spoon. Then use your hands to bring the dough together.

Reserve one-quarter of the dough to use for the lid. Roll out the remaining dough into a large circle on a lightly floured surface. Neatly line the tin with it, then fill the pastry case with the chickpea curry, pressing it down to level off the surface.

Roll the reserved piece of dough into a circle to fit the top of the pie. Brush the rim of the pastry case with beaten egg and lay the lid on top. Press the edges together to seal and trim off the excess dough. Make a slit in the top of the pie to allow steam to escape. Crimp the edges and decorate with dough trimmings as you like. Brush the pie well with beaten egg.

Bake for 30 minutes, then reduce the heat to 180°C (350°F), Gas Mark 4 and bake for another 40 minutes or until the pie is golden brown. Leave it to cool in the tin for 10 minutes, then transfer it to a plate to serve. This pie will keep, refrigerated, in an airtight container for up to 3 days. Warm it in an oven preheated to 180°C (350°F), Gas Mark 4 for 10 minutes before serving.

For comfort food I like nothing better than a delicious hot pie. This light puff pastry creation is filled with paneer and a beautiful blend of mustard seeds, turmeric, mango powder and other spices. The soft, crumbly, moist paneer absorbs the flavours of the spices, making a perfect match for the crisp pastry. Paneer is a fresh Indian cheese used in both sweet and savoury dishes. It is usually prepared in Indian homes by adding lemon juice or vinegar to milk, then separating the curds from the whey. In the UK it is often available at supermarkets. If you are not very fond of cheese, you can substitute boiled potatoes for the paneer for an equally delicious result.

Paneer pie

Serves 8–10

butter, for greasing

500g (1lb 2oz) ready-rolled puff pastry

plain flour, for dusting

1 egg, beaten

For the filling

2 tablespoons vegetable oil

1 tablespoon black mustard seeds

1 onion, finely chopped

$^1/_2$ teaspoon chilli powder

1 teaspoon garam masala

1 teaspoon ground turmeric

1 teaspoon mango powder (*amchur*)

2 x 225g (8oz) packets of paneer, roughly grated

salt

Start by making the filling. Heat the oil in a pan over a medium heat and, once it is hot, add the mustard seeds. As soon as they start to sizzle, put in the chopped onion and fry for a few minutes until softened. Add the chilli powder, garam masala, turmeric, mango powder and some salt, to taste. Fry for 1 minute, then add the grated paneer. Fry for another 5 minutes over a low heat until nicely cooked. Leave to cool.

Preheat the oven to 180°C (350°F), Gas Mark 4. Grease a 20cm (8in) round cake tin that is roughly 5cm (2in) deep.

Reserve a little puff pastry for the lid, then roll out the remaining puff pastry on a lightly floured surface until it is slightly larger than the size of your tin. Line the tin with the pastry, leaving the excess pastry overhanging the edge. Fill the pastry with the paneer mixture and level off the top surface of the filling, either with the back of a spoon or by hand. Brush the edge of the pastry with beaten egg.

Roll out the reserved pastry to the size of the tin and place it over the filling, then press the edges to seal the pie. Now trim off the excess pastry and, if you like, seal the edges in a pattern of our choice. Brush the lid with beaten egg and bake for 1¼ hours or until the pie is lovely and brown. Leave it to stand for few minutes before serving. This pie will keep, refrigerated, in an airtight container for up to 4 days. If you want to eat it warm, reheat it in an oven preheated to 180°C (350°F), Gas Mark 4 for 10 minutes.

This quick-and-easy puff pastry tart is inspired by a delicious curry of aubergines, tomatoes and onions that my mum makes. I have taken those flavours and added a bit of Cheddar to unite it all. The tart is great served with Coriander and Mint Chutney (*see* page 220) and Cucumber Raita (*see* page 232), or a simple salad.

Aubergine and onion tart

Serves 6–8

1 aubergine, cut into 5mm (¼in) slices

4 tablespoons olive oil

3 red onions, thinly sliced

325g (11½oz) ready-rolled puff pastry

plain flour, for dusting

4 tablespoons sun-dried tomato paste

½ teaspoon salt

50g (1¾oz) Cheddar cheese, grated

Preheat a griddle pan over a high heat until hot. Brush the aubergine with half the olive oil. Working in batches, griddle the aubergine slices for 4–5 minutes on each side until they are fully cooked and brown.

Heat the remaining olive oil over a medium heat. Stir in the red onions, then cover with a lid and cook for 8–10 minutes, stirring occasionally. Set aside to cool.

Preheat the oven to 200°C (400°F), Gas Mark 6. Unroll the pastry on a lightly floured baking tray. Gently score a line around the edge of the pastry, 1cm (½in) from the edge. Spread the tomato paste on the inner rectangle of pastry and cover with the cooked onions. Sprinkle with ¼ teaspoon of the salt. Neatly arrange the cooked aubergine slices on top and sprinkle with the remaining salt. Now sprinkle with the grated cheese. Bake for 25–30 minutes until the pastry is cooked and brown. Serve warm or cold. This tart is best eaten on the day it is made.

Sweet things

Rasgulla, the main ingredients of which are milk and sugar, are available in sweet shops across India, but are most popular in Western India. Although they are not often made in homes, that doesn't mean they are tricky to prepare – in fact, I believe you'll find them easy to make.

Saffron rasgulla

**Serves 6–8 people
(makes 20)**

1 litre (1³/₄ pints) milk

pinch of saffron threads

1 tablespoon lime juice

1 teaspoon water, plus 750ml (26fl oz)

250g (9oz) granulated sugar

1 tablespoon cornflour

In a saucepan, slowly bring the milk to the boil, then immediately take it off the heat and add the saffron. In a glass, mix the lime juice and the 1 teaspoon measured water together, then pour this mixture into the hot milk, stirring well. Leave to stand for 5 minutes.

Line a fine sieve with a muslin cloth and strain the curdled milk through it. Gather the cloth with the curds inside and squeeze out as much liquid as you can. Leave the bundle in the sieve and set the sieve over a jug. Place a small plate on top, then top this with a couple of produce cans, to weigh down the bundle (which helps press out the excess liquid). Allow the curds to drain for 15 minutes.

Meanwhile, in a wide pan, heat the sugar with the 750ml (26fl oz) measured water until the sugar has dissolved. Remove the syrup from the heat.

Remove the curd (also known as *cheena*) from the cloth. Place it on a clean work surface, sprinkle with the cornflour and knead with the palm of your hand for 10 minutes. The mixture starts off crumbly, but slowly comes together in a very soft dough. Roll the dough into a fat sausage and cut it into 20 pieces. Roll each into a smooth ball in your hands.

Once all the balls are ready, bring the syrup to the boil. Gently plop the balls into it, then cover and cook over a medium heat for 15 minutes. The *rasgulla* will double in size and become spongy and soft. Take the pan off the heat, leaving the *rasgulla* in the syrup until ready to serve. Serve warm or chilled with a drizzle of syrup. The *rasgulla* can be stored in the syrup, refrigerated, in an airtight container for up to 3 days.

Brownies are quick, easy to make and delicious – who doesn't love them? In India, whole roasted peanuts are very popular in both sweet and savoury cooking. I combine them with chocolate and peanut butter in this recipe for deliciously moreish brownies with a satisfying texture.

Peanut chocolate brownies

**Makes 20 small squares
or 12 large squares**

200g (7oz) golden caster sugar

200g (7oz) light muscovado sugar

4 large eggs

150g (5½oz) plain dark chocolate
(minimum 70 per cent cocoa solids)

110g (4oz) crunchy peanut butter

110g (4oz) unsalted butter

110g (4oz) self-raising flour

110g (4oz) roasted peanuts,
lightly crushed

vanilla ice cream, to serve
(optional)

Preheat the oven to 180°C (350°F), Gas Mark 4. Grease a 22–23cm (8½–9in) square brownie tin and line it with nonstick baking paper.

In a large bowl, whisk the sugars and eggs together with an electric whisk for 4–5 minutes until the mixture is pale and creamy.

Break the chocolate into a heatproof bowl, add the peanut butter and butter and set the bowl over a pan of steaming water until the mixture has melted, ensuring the base of the bowl doesn't touch the water beneath it. Pour the choc-nut mixture into the egg-and-sugar mixture and stir. Sift the flour straight into the same bowl, then add the crushed peanuts and mix well.

Pour the brownie batter into the prepared tin and bake for 20–25 minutes or until the top is crisp but the middle is still a bit gooey. Leave to cool in the tin for 10 minutes, then turn the cake out. Cut it into squares. These brownies can be enjoyed warm when fresh out of the oven (with vanilla ice cream, if liked) or cold. They will keep in an airtight container for 4–5 days.

These are a must-try! They're perfect for serving as a sweetmeat or petit fours. Dried figs are very popular in India and are used in both savoury and sweet dishes, but my dad enjoys them just as they are after dinner. For these macarons I pair them with chocolate, which has a similar rich, tangy flavour. The seeds add a lovely texture to the ganache and work well with the toasted hazelnuts sprinkled on the meringues.

Fig and chocolate macarons

Makes 40

170g (6oz) icing sugar

160g (5³/₄oz) ground almonds

3 egg whites (about 120ml/4fl oz)

1 teaspoon caramel gel food colour

15 drops of butterscotch extract

160g (5³/₄oz) caster sugar

50ml (2fl oz) water

handful of toasted blanched hazelnuts, chopped

For the ganache

300ml (¹/₂ pint) double cream

125g (4¹/₂oz) milk chocolate, chopped

125g (4¹/₂oz) plain dark chocolate (70 per cent cocoa solids), chopped

100g (3¹/₂oz) dried figs, very finely chopped

To make the macarons, sift the icing sugar and almonds into a bowl and mix well. Add half the egg whites and mix to form a thick paste. Add the caramel colouring and butterscotch extract and mix well. Set aside.

In a saucepan, gently heat the caster sugar and measured water until the sugar has completely dissolved, then bring to a simmer. Put a sugar thermometer in the pan and cook until the sugar syrup reaches 118°C (244°F). Once it has reached 115°C (239°F), start whisking the remaining egg whites in a stand mixer set to a high speed until soft peaks form. When the sugar syrup has reached 118°C (244°F), slowly pour it into the egg whites in the stand mixer, whisking continuously. Keep whisking on a high speed until the mixture has cooled down and the bowl is no longer hot.

Add this meringue to the almond-and-sugar mixture and mix well. Spoon into a piping bag fitted with a 1cm (¹/₂in) round piping nozzle, or use a disposable piping bag and cut off the tip to make a 1cm (¹/₂in) hole. Line 2 baking trays with nonstick baking paper and pipe 80 discs with the meringue mixture, each with a diameter of 2.5cm (1in). Sprinkle a few pieces of toasted hazelnut on each disc and tap the trays on the work surface to release air bubbles in the mixture. Leave to rest for 30 minutes until the discs form a skin and are no longer sticky.

Meanwhile, preheat the oven to 180°C (350°F), Gas Mark 4. Bake the macarons for 12 minutes or until dry and firm. Leave to cool on the baking paper. Gently peel them from the paper and set aside.

To make the ganache, bring the cream to scalding point in a saucepan. Put the chopped chocolate into a mixing bowl, pour the hot cream over it and mix well. Stir in the chopped figs and then, with a hand-held blender, blend the mixture, ensuring that the fig pieces are well incorporated into the chocolate cream. Leave the ganache to cool for a couple of hours.

To assemble, spoon the ganache into a disposable piping bag and cut off the tip to make a 5mm (¹/₄in) hole. Pipe the ganache on to the flat sides of half the macarons and sandwich with the remaining half. Serve immediately. These will keep in an airtight container for up to 2 days but are best eaten immediately.

I clearly remember helping my mum make this simple Indian shortbread when I was young – it would all be eaten up straight away! Nankhatai are very popular in India and readily available in all sorts of flavours, including nutmeg, coconut and lime, but cardamom is perhaps the most loved. Some people substitute besan (chickpea flour) for the semolina.

Nankhatai

Makes approximately 25

100g (3½oz) icing sugar, sifted
165g (5¾oz) plain flour
80g (2¾oz) semolina
¼ teaspoon bicarbonate of soda
¼ teaspoon ground cardamom
¼ teaspoon ground nutmeg
125g (4½oz) ghee, melted

Put all the dry ingredients in a large bowl and stir to combine. Slowly pour in the melted ghee, mixing well. Bring the mixture together in a dough and knead on a clean surface. Once you start kneading, the dough becomes very sticky and wet, but don't add any more flour. Knead for 8–10 minutes until the dough becomes a little pale. Use a dough scraper to help you transfer it to a bowl. Cover the dough with clingfilm, then cover the bowl with clingfilm, too. Leave to rest at room temperature for 1 hour.

Preheat the oven to 180°C (350°F), Gas Mark 4. Line 2 baking trays with nonstick baking paper.

Shape 1 tablespoon of the dough into a ball, place it on a prepared tray and flatten it slightly. Repeat with the remaining dough – you should have enough for about 25 biscuits. Bake for 15–20 minutes, then transfer to a wire rack and leave to cool. These biscuits will keep in an airtight container for up to 5 days.

Although these lovely mini cakes are simple to prepare, they look very impressive, making them ideal for a party or celebration. I think apricot goes really well with pomegranate. Using flaked almonds as well as juicy pomegranate seeds adds different dimensions of crunch to the meringue.

Pomegranate and apricot meringue cakes

Makes 6

100g (3¹/₂oz) unsalted butter, softened, plus extra for greasing
100g (3¹/₂oz) golden caster sugar
100g (3¹/₂oz) self-raising flour
2 large eggs
1 teaspoon vanilla extract

For the meringues

2 large egg whites
50g (1¾oz) caster sugar

For the decoration

6 tablespoons apricot jam
2 tablespoons flaked almonds
handful of pomegranate seeds

Preheat the oven to 180°C (350°F), Gas Mark 4. Grease 6 individual mini loose-based tart tins about 10cm (4in) in diameter.

In a large bowl, mix the butter, sugar, flour, eggs and vanilla extract together with an electric whisk for 2 minutes until the mixture is light and creamy. Pour the batter equally into the tart tins and bake for 10–12 minutes or until a skewer inserted into the centre of the cakes comes out clean.

Leave the cakes to cool in the tins for 10 minutes, then transfer to a baking tray. Trim a slice from the top of each of the cakes to make it level. Spread 1 tablespoon apricot jam evenly over the top of each cake.

In a large, very clean bowl, whisk the egg whites with an electric whisk until they form soft peaks. Slowly add the sugar, a little at a time, and continue whisking until the mixture turns shiny.

Put the meringue mixture into a disposable piping bag, cut off the tip and pipe it on to the cakes (or simply spoon it on to the cakes). Sprinkle with the flaked almonds and bake for another 10 minutes until golden.

Once baked, sprinkle the cakes with pomegranate seeds and serve warm or cold. Store these cakes in an airtight container for up to 3 days.

Crisp, flaky pastry leaves, crunchy cashews and almonds, sticky honey and the zingy blend of tea, fresh ginger, cloves and cardamom – this Asian twist on the famous Mediterranean pastry is easy to make and tastes sumptuous. It's great with a cup of mint tea in the afternoon.

Masala chai baklava

Makes 40

100g (3^1/$_2$oz) cashew nuts

100g (3^1/$_2$oz) almonds

^{1}/$_2$ teaspoon ground cardamom

250g (9oz) filo pastry (you will need 10 sheets)

125g (4^1/$_2$oz) unsalted butter, melted, plus extra for greasing

For the syrup

300g (10½oz) granulated sugar

200ml (⅓ pint) water

100ml (3^1/$_2$fl oz) clear honey

4 tea bags

seeds from 6 green cardamom pods

2.5cm (1in) piece of fresh root ginger, peeled and grated

6 cloves

Preheat the oven to 180°C (350°F), Gas Mark 4. Grease a 40cm × 30cm (16in × 12in) shallow baking tin.

Put all the syrup ingredients in a saucepan and bring to the boil. Reduce the heat and simmer for 10 minutes, stirring occasionally. Leave to cool for 10 minutes, then strain the syrup through a sieve and set aside.

To make the nutty filling, combine the cashews, almonds and ground cardamom in a food processor and pulse until finely chopped.

Gently unfold the filo and cover the sheets with a damp tea towel to prevent them drying out. Place 1 sheet of filo in the prepared baking tin and brush it all over with melted butter. Repeat twice more so that 3 sheets of buttery pastry are stacked in the baking tin. Sprinkle one-third of the nut mixture evenly all over the pastry. Now repeat this layering process twice more, then finish with a single layer of filo pastry and brush this all over with the remaining melted butter.

Using a very sharp knife, cut the baklava into diamond shapes, ensuring that the knife cuts right through the bottom layer. Bake for 30–35 minutes or until golden brown.

Remove from the oven and, while still warm, slowly spoon all the syrup evenly over the baklava. It is best to leave the baklava to sit at room temperature overnight before serving, which allows the pastry to absorb all the syrup, making it lovely and moist.

Indian sweets are made in small squares or rounds, like bite-sized desserts. I use this concept here to combine some of my favourite flavours. The bitterness of cocoa is highlighted by the coffee, and together they cut the sweetness of rose and cardamom – it's an absolute riot of flavours in one mouthful.

Rose, cardamom and coffee dessert slices

Makes approximately 25

200g (7oz) chocolate digestive biscuits

50g (1¾oz) unsalted butter, melted, plus extra for greasing

225ml (8fl oz) milk

1 teaspoon ground cardamom

1 tablespoon coffee granules

3 large egg yolks

75g (2¾oz) caster sugar

2 tablespoons cornflour

3 tablespoons cocoa powder

1 tablespoon boiling water

2 teaspoons powdered gelatine

250g (9oz) mascarpone cheese

1 teaspoon rosewater

white chocolate curls (or other decoration of your choice), to decorate

Preheat the oven to 180°C (350°F), Gas Mark 4. Grease a 20cm (8in) square cake tin and line it with nonstick baking paper.

Put the digestive biscuits in a plastic bag and bash them with a rolling pin to crush them to crumbs. Transfer the crumbs to a bowl and pour in the melted butter, mixing thoroughly so that the crumbs are completely coated. Tip the mixture into the prepared tin and press down firmly with the back of a spoon to create a smooth, even base layer. Bake for 15 minutes, then set aside to cool completely.

In a small pan, slowly heat the milk to scalding point. Add the ground cardamom and coffee granules and mix well, then remove the pan from the heat.

In a bowl, whisk the egg yolks, sugar, cornflour, cocoa and 2 tablespoons of the spiced milk together to form a smooth paste. Slowly add the remaining milk, whisking the whole time. Tip this mixture back into the saucepan and cook over a low heat for 2–3 minutes until it thickens enough to coat the back of a wooden spoon. Strain through a sieve into a clean bowl, cover with clingfilm and refrigerate for 10 minutes until lukewarm.

Put the measured boiling water in a small bowl and sprinkle in the gelatine. Stir until the gelatine powder has dissolved. Add this to the lukewarm pastry cream and mix well.

In another bowl, beat the mascarpone and rosewater together. Fold this into the pastry cream and pour the mixture over the biscuit base. Cover the tin with clingfilm and refrigerate overnight to set.

When ready to serve, carefully remove the cake from the tin and cut it into squares. To finish, sprinkle with white chocolate curls (or any decoration you prefer). The slices will keep, refrigerated, in an airtight container for up to 3 days.

Everyone knows savoury samosas, a very popular Indian snack, but did you realize there are also sweet samosas, filled with dried fruit, nuts or dairy products? Mine feature nuts and raisins and take a quick dip in sugar syrup after baking. They are crisp on the outside and crumbly on the inside, and perfect for the festive season.

Sweet baked samosas

Makes 24

For the pastry

400g (14oz) plain flour

pinch of salt

1/2 teaspoon baking powder

2 tablespoons golden caster sugar

100ml (3 1/2 fl oz) vegetable oil, plus extra for greasing and brushing

about 150ml (1/4 pint) water

For the filling

150g (5 1/2 oz) cashew nuts

150g (5 1/2 oz) almonds

100g (3 1/2 oz) raisins

2 tablespoons golden caster sugar

1 teaspoon ground cardamom

For the syrup

300g (10 1/2 oz) granulated sugar

100ml (3 1/2 fl oz) water

To make the pastry, combine the flour, salt, baking powder and sugar in a bowl. Mix the oil into the dry ingredients, then slowly add the measured water and stir to bring the pastry together – you might not need all of the water or you may need a bit more. Ensure that the pastry doesn't become wet or soggy. Knead it lightly on a clean surface for a minute, then transfer to a bowl, cover with clingfilm and leave to rest at room temperature for 30 minutes.

Meanwhile, prepare the filling. Coarsely grind the cashew nuts, almonds and raisins in a food processor.

Heat the oven to 180°C (350°F), Gas Mark 4. Lightly oil 2 baking trays.

Divide the pastry into 12 equal portions and roll each portion into a 17–18cm (6 1/2 –7in) circle with a thickness of about 2mm (1/16in). Cut each circle in half and brush the straight edge with a little water. Fold each semi-circle into a cone by bringing the straight edges together and pressing lightly to seal. Spoon 1 1/2 tablespoons of the filling into the pastry cone, brush the open rims with water and press together to seal. Place each samosa on a prepared baking tray and keep covered with a clean tea towel while you fill the remaining pastry.

Once all of the samosas are filled, brush them with a little oil and bake for 35–40 minutes until golden brown and crisp.

Meanwhile, make the sugar syrup. In a saucepan, heat the sugar and measured water together until the sugar dissolves. Simmer over a low heat for 6–8 minutes to make a thick syrup, then set aside.

Remove the samosas from the oven and transfer to a plate lined with kitchen paper to drain the excess oil. Then, taking 1 at a time, carefully dip each samosa in the sugar syrup to coat it completely, and place it on a wire rack to dry. Serve lukewarm or cold. These samosas will last in an airtight container for up to 5 days.

This is a simple and delicious dessert, proving that just a few ingredients, put together intelligently, can give a fantastic result. The bright flavours of mango and passion fruit make this pudding ideal for summer; topped with fragrant mint, it looks really fresh and light.

Mango and passion fruit baked yogurt

Serves 6

200ml (⅓ pint) natural yogurt
150ml (¼ pint) double cream
100ml (3½fl oz) condensed milk
100g (3½oz) mango purée
pulp of 1 passion fruit

For the decoration
6 tablespoons mango purée
6 mint leaves

Preheat the oven to 180°C (350°F), Gas Mark 4. In a bowl, combine the yogurt, cream, condensed milk, mango purée and passion fruit pulp and mix with a spatula until the ingredients are well blended.

Put the kettle on to boil. Transfer the mixture to a pouring jug and pour it equally into 6 shot glasses, ramekins, small glass bowls or cups. Put these into a deep roasting tray. Carefully fill the tray with hot water from the kettle so that it reaches halfway up the containers and place the tray in the oven. Bake for 12 minutes, then remove from the oven and leave the puddings in the tray of water to cool down.

Top each with 1 tablespoon mango purée and a mint leaf, then chill until ready to eat. Serve chilled. These servings will keep, refrigerated, for up to 3 days.

Pavlova is such a refreshing dessert. In this recipe, I use a couple of favourite Indian fruits – papaya and pomegranate – and combine them with the citrusy tang of passion fruit. Pistachios in the meringue give a great flavour balance to the whole glorious concoction.

Papaya, pomegranate and passion fruit pavlova

Serves 10–12

For the meringue
5 large egg whites
300g (10½oz) golden caster sugar
2 teaspoons cornflour
½ teaspoon vanilla bean paste
2 teaspoons cider vinegar
10 drops of passion fruit flavouring
50g (1¾oz) pistachio nuts, roughly chopped

For the topping
300ml (½ pint) double cream
2 tablespoons golden caster sugar
1 papaya, peeled, deseeded and sliced
seeds of 1 pomegranate
pulp of 2 passion fruits

Preheat the oven to 140°C (275°F), Gas Mark 1. Line a baking tray with nonstick baking paper.

First, make the meringue (do this on the day before serving, if you prefer). In a large, very clean bowl, whisk the egg whites with an electric whisk until soft peaks form. Slowly add the sugar, whisking continuously, until the mixture is shiny and thick.

In a small bowl, combine the cornflour, vanilla bean paste, cider vinegar and passion fruit flavouring and quickly whisk the mixture into the meringue. Fold in the chopped pistachios with a metal spoon.

Spoon the meringue mixture into a 22–25cm (8½–10in) circle on the prepared tray and swirl the edges. Bake for 1 hour until crisp, then turn off the oven and leave the pavlova in there to cool with the oven door propped ajar. Then transfer to an airtight container for storage, or to a serving plate when ready to serve.

When ready to serve, whisk the cream and sugar together until soft peaks form. Spoon the cream over the pavlova base. Scatter the papaya and pomegranate on top and drizzle with the pulp of the passion fruits. Once assembled, serve straight away, as the cream softens the meringue. The meringue will keep in an airtight container for up to 1 week.

I love steamed puddings. They are very light, yet so warming – perfect for cold days. This is a fresh-tasting version with sweet, warming undertones from the cinnamon and star anise. It's delicious with custard or simply fresh cream. I always use a regular vegetable steamer in which to cook puddings, but you can also put the pudding basin in a saucepan of boiling water, with the basin resting on a trivet set in the saucepan.

Rhubarb, strawberry and orange pudding with star anise and cinnamon

Serves 4–6

For the compote

100g (3½oz) rhubarb, chopped

finely grated zest and segmented flesh of 1 orange

60g (2¼oz) golden caster sugar

1 cinnamon stick

¼ teaspoon ground cinnamon

4 star anise

150g (5½oz) strawberries, hulled and halved

double cream, to serve

For the sponge

100g (3½oz) unsalted butter, softened, plus extra for greasing

100g (3½oz) golden caster sugar

100g (3½oz) self-raising flour

1 teaspoon baking powder

2 large eggs

Grease a 1-litre (1¾-pint) heatproof pudding basin. Lay a large sheet of nonstick baking paper on a similar-sized sheet of kitchen foil and, keeping them aligned, make a few pleats in the middle. Set aside.

To make the compote, put the rhubarb, orange zest and segments, sugar, cinnamon stick, ground cinnamon and star anise in a saucepan and cook over a low heat for 10 minutes. Take the pan off the heat and add the strawberries. Mix well and set aside to cool.

To make the sponge, mix all the ingredients in a large bowl with an electric whisk for 2 minutes or until light and creamy.

Remove the cinnamon stick and star anise from the compote, then spoon the mixture into the prepared pudding basin. Gently spoon the batter on top so as not to disturb the fruit. Lay the pleated foil and paper over the basin, foil-side up. Secure it to the neck of the pudding basin with kitchen string and form a handle that will allow you to safely lift the pudding out of the pan once it is cooked. Put the kettle on to boil.

Place a trivet in a saucepan, then sit the pudding basin on the trivet. Carefully pour hot water from the kettle into the saucepan so that it reaches halfway up the side of the pudding basin. (Alterntively, simply place the pudding basin, covered, directly in a steamer tray and set it over the steamer pan.) Cover tightly and cook over a low heat for 1¼ hours – you'll need to top up the simmering water halfway through the cooking time to ensure that the pan doesn't boil dry.

Carefully lift the basin from the pan and leave it to rest for 5 minutes, then remove the foil. Run a sharp knife around the edge of the pudding to help it slide out easily. Turn it out on to a warmed serving plate and serve hot. Once cooled, this pudding will keep, refrigerated, in an airtight container for up to 3 days. Reheat it in a microwave oven on a medium setting for a few seconds before serving with double cream drizzled on top.

My daughter and I love a good profiterole. In this recipe, I add the sweetness of star anise to the classic English combination of rhubarb and custard.

Star anise and rhubarb profiteroles

Serves 8–10

For the pastry

60g (2¼oz) unsalted butter

¼ teaspoon salt

1 teaspoon caster sugar

½ teaspoon ground star anise

125ml (4fl oz) water

85g (3oz) plain flour

2–3 large eggs, beaten

For the filling

250ml (9fl oz) milk

4 star anise

3 egg yolks

50g (1¾oz) caster sugar, plus 3 tablespoons

25g (1oz) plain flour, sifted

100g (3½oz) rhubarb, chopped

finely grated zest of 1 orange

juice of ½ orange

100ml (3½fl oz) double cream

Preheat the oven to 180°C (350°F), Gas Mark 4. Line 2 baking trays with nonstick baking paper. Draw 3–3.5cm (1¼in) circles on the paper (roughly 30 circles) as templates for the profiteroles, leaving enough space between each circle for the profiteroles to expand during cooking.

For the pastry, combine the butter, salt, sugar, star anise and measured water in a saucepan over a medium heat. Once the butter has melted, bring the liquid to the boil, then take the pan off the heat. Add the flour and quickly stir with a wooden spoon to form a dough. Heat over a low heat, stirring vigorously, for 2 minutes until the mixture comes away from the side of the pan. Tip into a large bowl and leave to cool until barely warm. Using an electric whisk, gradually add the beaten eggs to the paste, whisking well after each addition. You might not need all the egg, so towards the end, add it 1 tablespoon at a time until you have a shiny paste that falls from the spoon when lightly shaken. Spoon into a disposable piping bag, cut off the tip and pipe balls on to the templates drawn on the baking paper. Bake for 30 minutes.

Remove the baking trays from the oven and prick a small hole on the base of each pastry ball to let out the steam. Return to the oven and bake for a further 10 minutes or until firm. Transfer to a wire rack and leave to cool.

Make the filling. Put the milk and star anise in a saucepan and bring to the boil. In a mixing bowl, whisk together the egg yolks and the 50g (1¾oz) caster sugar with an electric whisk until pale and creamy. Add the flour and whisk again until smooth. Slowly add the infused milk, whisking the whole time. Pour back into the pan and cook over a very low heat for 4–5 minutes until it thickens, whisking the whole time. Remove the star anise. Pour the pastry cream into a clean bowl, cover the surface with clingfilm and chill. Preheat the oven to 180°C (350°F), Gas Mark 4. Put the rhubarb in a baking tray and sprinkle with 1 tablespoon caster sugar and the orange zest and juice. Bake for 20–25 minutes until soft. Whizz to a purée in a blender.

To finish the filling, whisk the double cream with the remaining 2 tablespoons of caster sugar in a large bowl until soft peaks form. Add the rhubarb purée and chilled pastry cream and fold it all together. Spoon into a clean disposable piping bag. Make a hole in the bottom of each pastry ball. Cut off the tip of the piping bag and fill each pastry generously with the rhubarb cream. Serve the profiteroles straight away. Once filled, these are best eaten the day they are made. The unfilled buns will keep in an airtight container for up to 3 days. If they become soft, reheat them in an oven preheated to 180°C (350°F), Gas Mark 4 for 5–7 minutes to crisp them up.

Star anise

Easily the prettiest spice, rust-coloured star anise is recognizable by its eight elegantly tapered pods or carpels – sometimes there may be as many as twelve or as few as six, but eight is the norm. Although they secrete seeds, the carpels are where most of the flavour resides. Star anise are the fruits of a tree that is related to the magnolia and is thought to hail from Southwest China and Northeast Vietnam. The vast majority of the world's production goes into anti-influenza medication, but star anise is also used to manufacture various alcoholic spirits and liqueurs.

Star anise and aniseed are not the same thing – the plants are unrelated, the latter originating in the Levant – but they do contain the same essential oil, which delivers a warm, slightly smoky, liquorice-like flavour and aroma.

Of course, star anise is best known for its use in Chinese cuisine. It is the dominant flavour in five-spice powder and an important inclusion in the red master stock used to braise duck and other birds. In fact, wherever it is in common use, cooks seem to agree that star anise works a treat with meat and poultry – think of Vietnamese pho or Malay chicken curries.

In Indian cuisine, star anise is usually added whole to the pan to give a subtle flavour to slow-cooked dishes, curries and rice dishes, including pulao and biryani. It is also frequently used in garam masala and masala chai (and also in the sweet, creamy iced tea of Thailand).

While I use star anise in chicken curries and rice dishes, just like my mum, I also love experimenting with ground star anise in sweet bakes. It works with many fruits – apple, banana, pear, orange and strawberry, for instance – and with fresh herbs, including basil and mint.

Next time you make carrot cake or a coffee and walnut cake, try adding a little ground star anise to lift them out of the ordinary. It is good with chocolate bakes, too, bringing a refreshing hit to cut the richness of the chocolate. Vanilla is another good match, so try adding a pinch of ground star anise with vanilla when whipping up a creamy cake filling or icing.

Recipes featuring star anise

Star anise and lemon chocolate mousse cake (*see* page 59)

Peach, star anise and almond tart (*see* page 66)

Rhubarb, strawberry and orange pudding with star anise and cinnamon (*see* page 113)

Star anise and rhubarb profiteroles (*see* page 114)

Star anise, date and chocolate bread (*see* page 197)

Brioche is one of my favourite breads. Although it takes quite a time to make, it is worth the effort, as these marvellous mouthfuls demonstrate. The little saffron-infused buns are filled with a luxurious mixture of cream cheese and pastry cream, and topped with crunchy green pistachios.

Saffron brioche buns with mango cardamom cream

Makes 20

2 pinches of saffron threads

70ml (2½fl oz) milk, warmed

250g (9oz) strong white bread flour, plus extra for dusting

5g (⅛oz) fast-action dried yeast

5g (⅛oz) salt

25g (1oz) caster sugar

2 large eggs, plus 1 large egg, beaten, for brushing

125g (4½oz) unsalted butter, softened

oil, for greasing

handful of pearl sugar

For the filling and decoration

250ml (9fl oz) milk

seeds from 6 green cardamom pods, lightly crushed

3 egg yolks

50g (1¾oz) caster sugar

25g (1oz) plain flour

75g (2¾oz) mango purée

100g (3½oz) cream cheese

handful of chopped pistachio nuts

In a small bowl, soak the saffron in the warmed milk and leave to infuse for 15 minutes.

Put the flour, yeast, salt, sugar and eggs in the bowl of a stand mixer fitted with a dough hook. Add the saffron milk and mix on a medium speed for 7–8 minutes. With the machine still running, gradually add the butter, then continue mixing for another 5 minutes until the butter is fully incorporated and the dough is soft.

Tip the dough into a clean bowl, cover with clingfilm and chill for 7 hours or overnight.

When ready to proceed, divide the dough into 20 portions. Roll them into small balls on a lightly floured surface and place on a floured baking tray, leaving enough space between them for the buns to expand. Cover with oiled clingfilm and leave to rise for 1–2 hours or until doubled in size.

Preheat the oven to 190°C (375°F), Gas Mark 5. Brush the buns lightly with beaten egg and sprinkle some pearl sugar on top. Bake for 15–20 minutes or until golden brown. Transfer the buns to a wire rack and leave to cool.

Meanwhile, prepare the filling. Slowly heat the milk and cardamom together in a saucepan. Remove from the heat once the milk starts to simmer.

In a bowl, whisk the egg yolks and sugar together with an electric whisk until pale and creamy. Sift in the flour and whisk well. Slowly incorporate the cardamom-infused milk, whisking the whole time. Return the mixture to the saucepan and cook over a low heat until smooth and thick, stirring constantly. Add the mango purée and mix well. Strain the pastry cream through a sieve into a clean bowl, cover the surface with clingfilm and chill.

Once the pastry cream has cooled, beat the cream cheese in a bowl until smooth, then add the pastry cream and mix well.

To assemble, slice each brioche bun in half. Spoon the filling into a disposable piping bag, cut off the tip and pipe it on to 1 side of the bun. Sprinkle chopped pistachios on top, cover with the other brioche half and serve.

Little round sweets called *laddoo* are served after dinner and during festivals in India. This delicious sugar-free version is a great healthy snack for kids and is easy and quick to make. The crunch of the dried figs works really well with all the different nut flavours and a hint of cardamom.

Sugar-free fig and nut laddoo

Makes 12

150g (5½oz) dried figs

20g (¾oz) cashew nuts, roughly chopped

20g (¾oz) almonds, roughly chopped

20g (¾oz) pistachio nuts, roughly chopped

¼ teaspoon ground cardamom

1 tablespoon ghee, melted

In a heatproof bowl, soak the figs in freshly boiled water for 15 minutes. Drain the water from the figs and blend them to a purée in a food processor.

Combine the fig purée, chopped nuts, ground cardamom and melted ghee in a bowl, mixing well with your hands. Roll the mixture into 12 small balls and put them on a plate to set. The laddoo will keep in an airtight container for up to 6 days.

I get very nostalgic about these crispy rolls filled with buttercream. My sisters and I loved eating them as children. Many Indian bakeries sell them, but we would go with my dad to a special one that baked them fresh every evening. On my last visit to my parent's house, we went back to that bakery and, to my surprise, they still sell them. Once you own the metal moulds, you will find cream horns are a no-fuss, simple bake that you make again and again.

Cream horns

Makes 6

For the pastry rolls

butter, for greasing

plain flour, for dusting

500g (1lb 2oz) puff pastry

1 egg, beaten with a pinch of salt

caster sugar, for sprinkling

For the buttercream

100g (3½oz) salted butter, softened

200g (7oz) icing sugar, sifted

½ teaspoon vanilla extract

1 tablespoon milk

Grease the outsides of 6 cream horn moulds and sprinkle generously with flour. Lightly flour a baking tray.

On a lightly floured surface, roll out the puff pastry to a rectangle measuring 45cm × 30cm (18in × 12in). Neatly trim the edges of the rectangle, then cut across the shorter length into 6 equal strips, each roughly 4–5cm (1½–2in) wide.

Wrap the pastry around the cone-shaped moulds, starting from the tip and moving upwards, carefully overlapping each coil of pastry by about one-third of its width. Once you have covered the mould, trim off the excess pastry. Brush all over with the beaten egg, then sprinkle with caster sugar. Put the moulded cones on the prepared baking tray and chill for 15 minutes.

Preheat the oven to 200°C (400°F), Gas Mark 6. Remove the moulded pastry cones from the refrigerator and bake for 20–25 minutes until golden brown and crispy. Sit them on a wire rack for 5 minutes until cool enough to handle, then remove the moulds and leave the pastry cones on the wire rack to cool completely.

To make the buttercream, in a bowl, whisk the butter, icing sugar, vanilla and milk together with an electric whisk for 1 minute until light and creamy. Spoon the buttercream into a piping bag fitted with a 1cm (½in) piping nozzle, or use a disposable piping bag and cut off the tip to make a 1cm (½in) hole.

Fill the pastry cones with the buttercream, piping it all the way from the tip at the base to the top. Serve straight away.

Everybody loves Swiss roll – the swirling layers of cream and cake are always a treat. I've updated the classic recipe with a touch of cardamom, which lends a citrus-like kick to the sponge, offsetting the juicy – and very pretty – fruit perfectly. It's summer on a plate!

Peach and strawberry Swiss roll

Serves 8–10

For the cake

4 large eggs

100g (3¹/₂oz) caster sugar, plus extra for sprinkling

100g (3¹/₂oz) strawberries, hulled

100g (3¹/₂oz) self-raising flour

¹/₂ teaspoon ground cardamom

For the filling and decoration

3 peaches, peeled (*see* page 66), stoned and thinly sliced

50g (1³/₄oz) unsalted butter, softened

70g (2¹/₂oz) caster sugar

¹/₂ teaspoon vanilla bean paste

300g (10¹/₂oz) double cream

4 tablespoons golden caster sugar

150g (5¹/₂oz) strawberries, hulled and finely chopped

Preheat the oven to 180°C (350°F), Gas Mark 4. Grease a 33cm × 23cm (13in × 9in) Swiss roll tin and line it with nonstick baking paper.

First make the cake. Whisk the eggs and sugar together with an electric whisk or a stand mixer fitted with a whisk attachment for 5–7 minutes until pale and thick and the mixture leaves a trail when the whisk is lifted from the bowl.

Pulse the strawberries in a food processor or blender just once, so that they are very finely chopped but not yet a purée. Add this to the egg mixture with the flour and cardamom and fold together, ensuring that you do not lose too much air from the mixture. Pour the batter into the prepared tin and bake for 12–15 minutes until the sponge bounces back when pressed. Leave to cool in the tin for 2 minutes.

Place a large sheet of nonstick baking paper on a work surface and sprinkle some caster sugar on top. Invert the Swiss roll tin to transfer the cake to the baking paper. Carefully peel away the paper. Roll up the cake tightly from a short edge and leave it rolled up to cool completely.

To make the filling, cook the peaches in the same Swiss roll tin. Put the butter, caster sugar and vanilla bean paste in the tray and place the tray in the oven for 2 minutes. When the butter has melted, remove the tray from the oven and mix well. Put the sliced peaches in the butter mixture, turning to coat them in the mixture. Bake for 10–12 minutes to cook the peaches slightly, then leave them in the butter mixture in the baking tray to cool completely.

Whisk the cream and golden caster sugar together in a bowl until medium-stiff peaks form. Peel and chop 4 slices of peach, then fold them into the cream along with the chopped strawberries. Unroll the cake and spread about two-thirds of the fruity cream across the top surface, keeping the edges clear. Roll up the cake and filling, then transfer the roll to a serving dish. Spoon the remaining cream on top and decorate with the remaining peach slices. Serve immediately. This roll will keep, refrigerated, in an airtight container for up to 3 days.

Serving these éclairs is the perfect way to finish a summer meal and they are easy and fun to bake! Mango works really well with hazelnut praline, which has richness and crunch, and the hint of lime in the pastry complements the chocolate caramel glaze.

Mango and praline éclairs

Makes 12–14

For the pastry

60g (2¼oz) unsalted butter

¼ teaspoon salt

1 teaspoon caster sugar

finely grated zest of 1 lime

125ml (4fl oz) water

85g (3oz) plain flour

2–3 large eggs, beaten, plus
1 large egg, beaten, for brushing

For the praline

50g (1¾oz) caster sugar

50g (1¾oz) hazelnuts, chopped

oil, for greasing

For the filling

300ml (½ pint) double cream

150g (5½oz) mascarpone cheese

1 tablespoon caster sugar

75g (2¾oz) mango purée

For the chocolate glaze

60g (2¼oz) dark muscovado sugar

30g (1oz) unsalted butter

20g (¾oz) plain dark chocolate
(minimum 70 per cent cocoa
solids), chopped

1 tablespoon double cream

Preheat the oven to 180°C (350°F), Gas Mark 4. Line 2 baking trays with nonstick baking paper.

For the pastry, put the butter, salt, sugar, lime zest and measured water in a saucepan over a medium heat. Once the butter has melted, bring the mixture to the boil and immediately remove the pan from the heat. Add the flour and quickly stir with a wooden spoon to form a dough. Put the pan back over a low heat and stir vigorously for 2 minutes until the paste comes away from the side of the pan. Tip the paste into a large bowl and leave to cool until barely warm. Using an electric whisk, gradually add the beaten eggs to the cooled paste, whisking well after each addition. You might not need all the egg so, towards the end, add only 1 tablespoon at a time until the mixture becomes a shiny paste that falls from the spoon when lightly shaken.

Spoon the paste into a piping bag fitted with a 1.5cm (⅝in) round nozzle, or use a disposable piping bag and cut off the tip to make a 1.5cm (⅝in) hole. Pipe 12–14 lines, each 10cm (4in) long, on to the trays. Brush with the beaten egg and bake for 25–30 minutes. Remove the trays from the oven and make a hole at one end of each éclair to let out the steam. Bake for a further 10 minutes until golden brown and crisp. Cool on a wire rack.

To make the praline, heat the sugar and hazelnuts in a saucepan over a low heat until the sugar has caramelized; keep stirring to ensure that the nuts are coated with sugar. Spread the caramelized nuts on a lightly oiled nonstick baking paper and leave to cool. Once cool, put the praline between 2 sheets of nonstick baking paper and crush with a rolling pin. Set aside.

Now make the filling. In a bowl, whisk the cream, mascarpone and sugar together until soft peaks form. Fold 4 tablespoons of the crushed praline into this cream (reserve the remainder) along with the mango purée. Spoon into a disposable piping bag and cut off the tip. Cut the éclairs in half horizontally. Pipe the flavoured cream on to the bottom halves. Sprinkle with a little of the reserved crushed praline and cover with the top halves.

For the chocolate glaze, heat the sugar and butter together in a saucepan. Bring the mixture to the boil, stirring, for 1 minute. Remove from the heat, add the chocolate and stir until it has melted. Add the cream and mix well. Carefully drizzle the hot glaze on top of the éclairs and sprinkle a bit more crushed praline on top. The glaze will set on cooling. Keep the éclairs chilled until ready to eat. Once they are filled, these are best eaten the same day.

Black sesame is used quite a lot in sweet and savoury cooking in India, although some may associate it more with Japan, which is also known for matcha green tea. I love the way sesame and matcha go together, and a mix of dark and milk chocolate finishes these wafer-thin biscuits perfectly.

Black sesame and matcha tuiles

Makes 18–20

110g (4oz) caster sugar

110g (4oz) plain flour

2 large egg whites

2 teaspoons matcha green tea powder

110g (4oz) unsalted butter, melted

2 tablespoons black sesame seeds

100g (3½oz) milk chocolate

100g (3½oz) plain dark chocolate (minimum 70 per cent cocoa solids)

In a bowl, whisk the sugar, flour, egg whites and green tea powder together until smooth. Add the melted butter and sesame seeds and whisk again until thoroughly combined. Cover the bowl with clingfilm and chill for 30 minutes.

Preheat the oven to 180°C (350°F), Gas Mark 4. Line 2 baking trays with nonstick baking paper.

Draw 10cm (4in) diameter circles on the paper. Spoon 1 teaspoon of the tuile mixture into the centre of each circle and use the back of a spoon to spread it out to the size of the circles you've drawn. Bake for 8–10 minutes. As soon as the tuiles are out of the oven, lift them with a palette knife and drape them over a rolling pin. Leave them on the rolling pin to cool and harden.

Once the tuiles have cooled, break the chocolate into 2 separate heatproof bowls and set each of these over a pan of steaming water until the chocolate has melted, ensuring that the base of each bowl doesn't touch the water beneath it. While the chocolate is still warm, drizzle a little of each chocolate over the tuiles and leave to set. These tuiles will keep in an airtight container for up to 4 days.

Clove

Clove is so often associated with traditional British cooking – hot cross buns, mulled wine – one can easily forget how frequently it is used in other cuisines. The tiny dried buds of a type of myrtle tree native to Indonesia, cloves give a warming base note to many types of dishes. It is always used in small quantities, because its sweet, aromatic flavour is very strong and pungent.

In Indian cuisine, cloves are a typical component of garam masala and feature in many curries, particularly meat ones such as Kashmir's rogan josh and Bengal's *mangshor jhol*. They lend a rich flavour that is especially suited to winter. Marinades and spice mixes for kebabs are other ways in which cloves are paired with meat and poultry.

Two of India's best-loved pickles, mango and aubergine (*brinjal*), often feature cloves. Cloves are used in drinks, too – for example, masala chai and *nimbu pani*, a type of Indian lemonade – but rarely will you find them in Indian desserts.

I think cloves are underrated and use them a lot. The flavour goes well with tomatoes and onions.

I add cloves to an onion pulao, as their pungency is a great match for the sweetness of fried onions. When making a curry, start by frying a few cloves in a little oil with a cinnamon stick, bay leaves and green cardamom pods and you will find that the flavours come together like magic.

Clove and orange is a classic match, as is clove and apple (think of apple pies), but it works beautifully with other fruits, including peaches, blueberries and bananas or plantain. Ground clove is an essential component of American pumpkin pie spice mix and traditional European cookies such as *pfeffernüsse* and *lebkuchen*, so don't hesitate to try it in biscuits, gingerbreads, cakes and pie fillings.

Clove is a great spice to use, but it's rather underrated. Pairing it with cinnamon – as in Christmas mince pies and mulled wine, or a festive biryani – gives a touch of magic to these lovely cookies. Chocolate and pistachio nuts add creaminess. I think you'll find everything comes together beautifully.

Clove, cinnamon and chocolate cookies

Makes 40

175g (6oz) unsalted butter, softened

200g (7oz) dark muscovado sugar

75g (2¾oz) caster sugar

½ teaspoon ground cinnamon

¼ teaspoon ground cloves

1 large egg

1 egg yolk

250g (9oz) self-raising flour

175g (6oz) chocolate chips

175g (6oz) pistachio nuts, roughly chopped

Preheat the oven to 180°C (350°F), Gas Mark 4. Line 2 baking trays with nonstick baking paper.

Cream the butter, sugars and spices together with an electric whisk or in a stand mixer fitted with a paddle attachment until light and creamy. Mix in the whole egg and yolk. Now add the flour, chocolate chips and all but a handful of the chopped pistachios and mix to bring the dough together.

Roughly shape a big tablespoonful of the mixture into a ball and put a few of the reserved chopped pistachios on top. Place this ball on a lined baking tray and repeat with the remaining dough, leaving enough space between them for the cookies to spread during cooking. Bake for 12–15 minutes or until the cookies start to colour but are still chewy in the middle. Transfer to a wire rack to cool. These cookies will keep in an airtight container for up to 7 days.

The combination of almonds, cashews and raisins is very common in Indian puddings – think of *halwa* and *kheer*. For this very simple recipe I combine them with beautifully crisp puff pastry, plus some cardamom and cinnamon, which works very well.

Nut and spice palmiers

Makes 16

50g (1³/₄oz) cashew nuts

50g (1³/₄oz) almonds

50g (1³/₄oz) raisins

¹/₂ teaspoon ground cinnamon

¹/₂ teaspoon ground cardamom

50g (1³/₄oz) golden caster sugar, plus extra for sprinkling

50g (1³/₄oz) unsalted butter, melted

375g (13oz) ready-rolled puff pastry

1 egg, beaten

plain flour, for dusting

In a small food processer, finely grind the cashews, almonds and raisins with the cinnamon and cardamom. Transfer to a mixing bowl, add the sugar and melted butter and stir to make a paste.

Unroll the puff pastry sheet. Brush beaten egg all over it, then spread the nut paste evenly over the pastry sheet. Fold the longer edge of pastry into the middle, then bring in the opposite side so that the long edges meet along the centre line. Now fold in from each side again to create a layered length. Place the pastry roll on a floured baking tray and chill for 30 minutes.

Preheat the oven to 200°C (400°F), Gas Mark 6. Line 2 baking trays with nonstick baking paper. Remove the pastry roll from the refrigerator and cut it into 1cm (½in) slices. Lay them on the prepared baking trays. Brush with beaten egg and sprinkle some sugar on top.

Bake the palmiers for 10–15 minutes or until cooked through and golden. Transfer to a wire rack to cool. These palmiers will keep in an airtight container for up to 3 days.

In the winters when I was little, we would sit around as a family with bowls of pine nuts in their shells and spend ages peeling and eating them. Pine nuts are not much used in Indian cooking, but are frequently eaten on their own during festivals. They are great combined with coconut and almonds, which lend a creamy, chewy texture to these cookies.

Coconut and pine nut cookies

Makes 20

85g (3oz) unsalted butter, softened

110g (4oz) light muscovado sugar

50g (1³⁄₄oz) golden caster sugar

1 teaspoon vanilla extract

1 egg yolk

100g (3¹⁄₂oz) self-raising flour

25g (1oz) ground almonds

50g (1³⁄₄oz) desiccated coconut

40g (1¹⁄₂oz) pine nuts

Preheat the oven to 180°C (350°F), Gas Mark 4. Line 2 baking trays with nonstick baking paper.

In a bowl, cream the butter, sugars and vanilla extract together with an electric whisk for a couple of minutes or until light and creamy. Add the egg yolk and mix well. Now add the flour, almonds and coconut and bring the dough together with your hands.

Shape 1 tablespoon of cookie dough into a ball and place it on a lined tray, then repeat with the remaining dough, leaving enough space between the balls on the trays for the cookies to spread during cooking. Bake for 15–20 minutes until the edges of the cookies start to brown but the middles remain slightly chewy. Transfer to a wire rack to cool. These cookies will keep in an airtight container for up to 5 days.

A great bake for kids, this very simple cookie recipe will become a firm favourite in no time. I use dates for their chocolaty flavour, and for these cookies you can use inexpensive cooking dates or more premium varieties, as you prefer. The oats add a lovely taste and texture.

Date and oat cookies

Makes 20–22

150g (5½oz) unsalted butter, softened

40g (1½oz) light soft brown sugar

80g (2¾oz) caster sugar

¼ teaspoon vanilla bean paste

1 egg yolk

175g (6oz) self-raising flour

25g (1oz) porridge oats

100g (3½oz) pitted dates, finely chopped

Preheat the oven to 180°C (350°F), Gas Mark 4. Line 2 baking trays with nonstick baking paper.

In a bowl, whisk the butter, sugars, vanilla bean paste and egg yolk together with an electric whisk until light and creamy. Fold in the flour, oats and dates with a metal spoon. Use your fingers to press the mixture together into a soft dough.

Roll 1 tablespoon of the dough into a ball. Flatten slightly and place it on a prepared baking tray, then repeat with the remaining dough, leaving enough space between the discs for the cookies to spread during cooking. The mixture should yield 20–22 cookies. Bake for 12–15 minutes until the edges start to colour but the middles are still gooey. These cookies will keep in an airtight container for up to 4 days.

A bright, fresh-tasting biscuit that's ideal for summer tea times. The lemony notes of coriander seeds add real oomph to lemon curd, which squares up to the sour tang of the raspberry biscuits. If your supermarket doesn't stock freeze-dried raspberry powder, search online; it is readily available from specialist stores for chefs as well as some health food shops.

Raspberry biscuits with lemon coriander curd

Makes 20

For the lemon coriander curd

finely grated zest and juice of 2 large lemons

2 tablespoons coriander seeds

100g (3½oz) caster sugar

pinch of salt

20g (¾oz) cornflour

3 egg yolks, beaten

25g (1oz) unsalted butter, softened

For the biscuits

80g (2¾oz) unsalted butter, softened

80g (2¾oz) caster sugar

2 tablespoons milk

2 teaspoons freeze-dried raspberry powder

¼ teaspoon vanilla bean paste

150g (5½oz) self-raising flour, sifted

60g (2¼oz) custard powder

To make the curd, put the lemon zest and juice, coriander seeds, sugar, salt and cornflour in a saucepan and heat gently until the sugar dissolves. Bring to the boil, then immediately take the pan off the heat. Stir in the egg yolks, then set the pan over a very low heat, whisking continuously. Cook for 3–4 minutes, whisking all the time, until the mixture is nice and thick.

Take the pan off the heat and whisk in the butter until it is fully incorporated. Strain the curd through a sieve into a clean bowl and leave to cool.

Preheat the oven to 180°C (350°F), Gas Mark 4. Line 2 baking trays with nonstick baking paper.

To make the biscuits, in a bowl, cream the butter and sugar together with an electric whisk until the mixture is light and creamy. Add the milk, raspberry powder and vanilla and beat until well combined. Add the sifted flour and custard powder and mix to a soft dough.

Roll 1 tablespoon of the dough into a ball and place it on a prepared tray. Repeat with the remaining mixture – you should have around 20 balls. Use the back of a small measuring spoon to make an indentation in each ball. Fill each hole with ½ teaspoon of the lemon coriander curd. (Any leftover curd will keep, refrigerated, in an airtight container for up to 3–4 weeks.) Bake the filled biscuits for 15 minutes. Transfer to a wire rack and leave to cool. These biscuits will keep in an airtight container for up to 4 days.

Whether in *laddoos* (a type of sweet) or cardamom *kheer* (rice pudding), the combination of coconut and cardamom is very popular in India. I wanted to apply it to these very light doughnuts, sumptuously filled with scented pastry cream and flecked with toasted coconut. The dough is quite sticky, so use a stand mixer for ease.

Coconut and cardamom doughnuts

Makes 20

500g (1lb 2oz) strong white bread flour, plus extra for dusting

7g (¹/₅oz) sachet fact-action dried yeast

10g (¹/₃oz) salt

60g (2¹/₄oz) caster sugar

4 large eggs

about 150ml (¹/₄ pint) water

125g (4¹/₂oz) unsalted butter, softened

vegetable oil, for greasing and deep-frying

For the filling

250ml (9fl oz) milk

1¹/₂ teaspoons ground cardamom

¹/₂ teaspoon vanilla extract

3 egg yolks

50g (1³/₄oz) caster sugar

25g (1oz) plain flour, sifted

600ml (20fl oz) double cream

For the coating

75g (2³/₄oz) desiccated coconut

100g (3¹/₂oz) icing sugar, sifted

To make the dough, put the flour in the bowl of a stand mixer fitted with a dough hook. Add the yeast and salt on opposite sides of the bowl. To this, add the sugar and eggs, then switch the stand mixer on to a medium speed setting and slowly add the measured water while the dough comes together – you might not need all the measured water or you might need a bit more. Knead for 8–10 minutes. Once the dough is smooth, slowly add the butter, mixing all the while. Knead for another 5 minutes until the dough is smooth and stretchy. Lightly oil a clean bowl, put the dough in it and cover with clingfilm. Leave to rise for 2 hours or until doubled in size.

Divide the dough into 20 portions and roll them into neat balls in the palms of your hands. Position them on 2–3 very well floured baking trays, allowing plenty of room around them for the doughnuts to expand, and place the trays inside oiled plastic bags. Leave to prove for another hour or until doubled in size.

While the dough is proving, prepare the filling. Put the milk in a saucepan with ½ teaspoon of the cardamom and the vanilla. Slowly bring the milk to scalding point.

In a mixing bowl, whisk the egg yolks and sugar together until light and creamy. Add the sifted flour and whisk again until smooth.

Slowly pour the hot milk into the egg mixture, whisking continuously. Return the mixture to the saucepan set over a medium heat and whisk until it comes to the boil. Reduce the heat to low and cook the pastry cream for another 5 minutes until thick, whisking continuously. Pour into a shallow dish, cover the surface with clingfilm and refrigerate to cool it.

To make the coating, lightly toast the desiccated coconut in a dry pan for 2–3 minutes, then tip it into a shallow tray and stir in the sugar. Transfer 6 tablespoons of this mixture to a large mixing bowl, leaving the rest on the tray ready to coat the doughnuts.

Add the double cream and remaining teaspoon of cardamom to the bowl of reserved sugar and coconut and whisk until the mixture forms soft peaks. Fold in the cooled pastry cream. Fit a piping bag with a 1cm (½in) piping nozzle and spoon the filling mixture into the bag.

Pour vegetable oil into a tall saucepan to a depth of one-third (or use a deep-fat fryer and follow the manufacturer's instructions). Heat the oil over a medium heat to 150°C (302°F). Carefully add 1–2 doughnuts and cook for 1½ minutes on each side. Transfer directly to the tray of sugar-and-coconut coating and turn to coat completely. Repeat with the remaining doughnuts, then leave them to cool.

Make a slit on 1 side of each doughnut and fill generously with the scented pastry cream. Eat as soon as possible. These doughnuts will keep for a day in an airtight container.

Syrupy rose and cardamom-flavoured *gulab jamuns* are a beloved Indian sweet and are sold in all Asian sweet shops. Here, I combine the best qualities of *gulab jamuns* and doughnuts to make a treat that, in my home, disappears faster than chocolate!

Gulab jamun doughnuts

Makes 60–70

250g (9oz) strong white bread flour, plus extra for dusting

5g (1/8oz) salt

5g (1/8oz) fast-action dried yeast

25g (1oz) caster sugar

2 tablespoons milk powder

1 teaspoon rosewater

1 teaspoon ground cardamom

2 large eggs

2 tablespoons warm milk

vegetable oil, for greasing and deep-frying

For the syrup

70g (2½oz) unsalted butter

200g (7oz) icing sugar

1/2 teaspoon rosewater

1/2 teaspoon ground cardamom

4 tablespoons boiling water

Put the flour, salt, yeast, sugar, milk powder, rosewater, cardamom, eggs and warm milk in a mixing bowl and bring the mixture together with your hands to make a dough. Knead the dough on a lightly oiled work surface for 8–10 minutes. Place it in an oiled bowl, cover with clingfilm and set aside to rise for 2–3 hours or until the dough has doubled in size.

Roll out the dough on a lightly floured surface to a thickness of 2–3mm (1/16–1/8in). Cut out circles using a 3–4cm (1¼–1½in) cookie cutter. Bring the remnants together, roll out again and cut out more circles. This quantity of dough will yield 60–70 discs. Arrange on lightly floured baking trays and put each tray into an oiled plastic bag. Leave to prove for 1 hour.

Prepare the syrup just before frying the doughnuts. Combine all the ingredients in a shallow pan over a low heat and whisk until the sugar has dissolved and the syrup is smooth.

Pour vegetable oil into a tall saucepan to a depth of one-third (or use a deep-fat fryer and follow the manufacturer's instructions). Heat the oil slowly to 150°C (302°F). Fry the doughnuts, in batches, for 1–2 minutes on each side until golden brown. Drain on a plate lined with kitchen paper, then gently pop them into the syrup, turning so that they are well coated, and leaving them to steep in the syrup while you fry the next batch. Then set the sticky doughnuts aside while the next batch is soaking. Serve warm or cold. These doughnuts will keep in an airtight container for up to 4 days.

Cinnamon

To the British, cinnamon is the quintessential sweet spice and most
people have a jar of ground cinnamon in the cupboard for baking.
I did not know of it until I moved to the UK. In India, my mother
used whole cinnamon sticks, and only for savoury dishes. That is
one of the great things about cinnamon – it works well in
both sweet and savoury cooking.

Cinnamon's flavour is warm, strong, spicy and intriguingly bitter, given its renowned sweetness. I like it with tomatoes, potatoes and fresh herbs. It blends well with other spices such as cardamom, star anise, cloves and ginger, and is a key ingredient in masala chai as well as the classic English baking blend known as mixed spice.

There are several types of cinnamon but the best is from Sri Lanka, where only the dried inner bark of *Cinnamomum verum*, a type of laurel, is used to produce the sticks. This tree also grows well in the Seychelles and Madagascar. The best cinnamon scrolls or quills are yellowish brown with thin, slightly pliable layers. Scrolls from China or Indonesia are darker coloured, with much thicker bark. Ready-ground cinnamon tends to be made from these coarser varieties, which have a bolder flavour.

Cinnamon goes well with almonds and walnuts, and brings wonderful depth to fruit dishes, especially those featuring bananas, figs, strawberries, oranges, apples and pears. You can use the quills as swizzle sticks for hot drinks including coffee, tea, cocoa, apple juice or mulled wine or cider.

In cooking, recipes often suggest a specific length of cinnamon stick, or breaking up sticks to release more flavour. The pieces are not meant to be eaten, so pick them out before serving or make sure they are presented as a garnish.

These flavourful sandwich biscuits are light yet indulgent. And they are easily varied, too – switch the hazelnuts to pistachios, almonds or chocolate sprinkles, and replace the nutmeg with cinnamon or cardamom. Have fun experimenting. I like the way nutmeg works with the flavours of cocoa and coffee.

Nutmeg and coffee biscuits

Makes 10

125g (4¹/₂oz) unsalted butter, softened

50g (1³/₄oz) icing sugar, sifted

100g (3¹/₂oz) plain flour

80g (2³/₄oz) self-raising flour

2 tablespoons cocoa powder

¹/₄ teaspoon ground nutmeg

50g (1³/₄oz) toasted hazelnuts, chopped, to decorate

For the filling

75g (2³/₄oz) unsalted butter, softened

100g (3¹/₂oz) icing sugar, sifted

1 teaspoon coffee extract

Preheat the oven to 180°C (350°F), Gas Mark 4. Line 2 baking trays with nonstick baking paper.

To make the biscuits, cream the butter and sugar together with an electric whisk for 2 minutes until the mixture is pale and creamy. Using a metal spoon, fold in the flours, cocoa powder and nutmeg and mix to a soft dough.

Roll 1 tablespoon of the dough into a ball, then repeat with the remaining dough – you should have about 20 balls. Use the base of a glass to press them down into 4cm (1¹/₂in) discs. Place these on the prepared baking trays and bake for 10 minutes. Transfer the biscuits to a wire rack to cool completely.

To make the filling, whisk the butter, icing sugar and coffee extract together in a bowl until light and creamy.

Using ³/₄ teaspoon per biscuit, spread the coffee cream on the flat sides of half the biscuits. Sandwich with the remaining biscuits. Use a spatula to spread a little more coffee cream around the joins.

Spread the chopped hazelnuts out on a plate. Roll the edges of the biscuits in the nuts to coat the circumferences. Store in an airtight container for up to 2 days.

This dessert does not contain any spices, yet still it reminds me of India. Peanuts are widely used in Indian cooking, for both sweet and savoury dishes, and in winter in particular they are made into peanut brittle, which is eaten as a sweet after meals. Peanut brittle epitomizes cold-weather comfort food. It is sold in shops and street stalls everywhere and is often made at home. In this dish, the nutty, toffee flavours of peanuts add richness to a light, fluffy meringue roulade and give it an enticing crunch.

Peanut meringue roulade

Serves 8–10

oil, for greasing

For the meringue

4 egg whites

200g (7oz) caster sugar

50g (1¾oz) roasted peanuts, finely chopped

For the peanut brittle and filling

175g (6oz) caster sugar

6 tablespoons water

100g (3½oz) roasted peanuts

300ml (½ pint) double cream

couple of handfuls of roughly chopped roasted peanuts

Heat the oven to 180°C (350°F), Gas Mark 4. Line a 25cm × 38cm (10in × 15in) shallow baking tin with nonstick baking paper.

To prepare the meringue, in a large, very clean bowl, whisk the egg whites with an electric whisk until soft peaks form. Slowly add the sugar, 1 tablespoon at a time, until you have a stiff and glossy mixture. Now lightly fold in the chopped peanuts. Spread the mixture evenly on the prepared tin. Bake for 20–25 minutes until nice and golden.

Place a large sheet of nonstick baking paper on the work surface. Once the meringue is cooked, invert the baking tin to transfer the meringue to the baking paper. Carefully peel away the baking paper, then leave the meringue to cool completely.

To make the peanut brittle, heat the sugar and measured water in a saucepan over a medium-low heat. Cook until the mixture becomes a caramel. Take the pan off the heat and add the peanuts. Spread the mixture on a lightly oiled sheet of nonstick baking paper and leave it to cool completely. Once cool, break the peanut brittle into pieces and grind these to a coarse powder in a food processor.

To make the filling, whisk the cream in a bowl until soft peaks form. Fold in 3 tablespoons of the ground brittle. Spread the cream on top of the cooled meringue, leaving the edges clear. Sprinkle a handful of the chopped peanuts over the cream.

Start rolling the meringue from a short side of the rectangle, using the baking paper to help you. Carefully transfer the roll to a serving plate. Sprinkle with a small handful of the remaining chopped peanuts and ground brittle. This roulade is best eaten straight after assembly.

Savoury
small bites

My mum makes these light, crispy snacks a lot. They are great fun and simple to make. She named them *karela papdi* because they look like *karela* (bitter gourd). They keep for quite a few days in an airtight container, so stock up – you won't be able to stop eating them! Serve them with a cup of tea and a chutney of your choice.

Karela papdi

Makes 24

300g (10½oz) plain flour

³/₄ teaspoon salt

¹/₂ teaspoon carom seeds

1 teaspoon smoked paprika

1 teaspoon mango powder (*amchur*)

vegetable oil, plus extra for deep-frying

130ml (4¹/₄fl oz) water

Combine the flour, salt, carom, smoked paprika, *amchur* and oil in a bowl and mix well. Slowly add the measured water, mixing to form a dough. Transfer the dough to a clean bowl, cover with clingfilm and leave to rest at room temperature for 30 minutes.

Divide the dough into 24 portions, each weighing about 20g (¾oz). Roll out each piece into a 10cm (4in) circle. Use a knife to score on the top surface a series of straight lines, leaving a 1cm (½in) rim and 1cm (½in) between each cut. Bring the edges of each circle together to bend it into the shape of a wrapped sweet, keeping the cuts loose. Press the edges together to join.

Pour vegetable oil into a tall saucepan to a depth of one-third (or, use a deep-fat fryer and follow the manufacturer's instructions). Heat the oil over a medium heat until a breadcrumb sizzles and turns brown when dropped into it. Once it is hot, carefully fry the *papdi*, in batches, for 2–3 minutes on each side. Remove and drain on kitchen paper, then leave to cool. These snacks will keep in an airtight container for up to 10 days.

When sweetcorn is in season, my mum makes delicious corn cakes with fresh herbs to cheer up rainy days. For this recipe, I use a similar mixture to fill filo rolls, which produces a light, crispy snack that makes wonderful finger food for a party or barbecue. Serve these rolls hot with a chutney of your choice.

Corn rolls

Makes 14

250g (9oz) filo pastry
(about 14 sheets)
100g (3½oz) unsalted butter,
melted

For the filling

340g (11¾oz) can sweetcorn,
drained
2.5cm (1in) piece of fresh root
ginger, peeled and finely grated
1 green chilli, finely chopped
handful of fresh coriander leaves,
finely chopped
1 teaspoon ground cumin
½ teaspoon salt
1 tablespoon lemon juice
pinch of granulated sugar

Combine all the filling ingredients in a bowl and mix well.

Preheat the oven to 200°C (400°F), Gas Mark 6.

Unfold the filo sheets and take 1 sheet to work with. Cover the rest with a clean, damp tea towel to prevent them drying out while you make each roll. Brush the sheet of filo lightly with melted butter and fold it in half. Brush again with butter and fold again in the opposite direction. Spoon 1 heaped tablespoon of the sweetcorn mixture along one long edge of the folded pastry and fold a little pastry over the filling. Tuck in the corners, then loosely roll up to form a cigar. Repeat with the remaining ingredients.

Place the filo rolls slightly apart on a baking tray and brush with melted butter. Bake for 15–17 minutes until golden and crisp. Serve straight away.

Flavour-packed *papdi chaat* is a savoury biscuit topped with potatoes and chutney. A popular snack in India, it is often made at home and commonly sold as street food. The biscuits go down a treat as a canapé to serve with drinks at a party or as a quick bite to eat with family or friends. There are many permutations of ingredients, both for the biscuits and the chutneys to spread on top. In this version, the sweet, slightly nutty flavour of dried fenugreek leaves (*kasuri methi*) combines with thyme-like carom seeds to create an exquisite biscuit, which is given extra punch by the chilli chutney. I have made this recipe a bit healthier than traditional versions by baking the biscuits instead of frying them. The *sev* (gram flour noodles) are available from some supermarkets and online Asian grocery shops.

Fenugreek papdi chaat

Makes 40–50

For the biscuits

300g (10½oz) plain flour, plus extra for dusting

50g (1¾oz) semolina

1 teaspoon salt

3 tablespoons dried fenugreek leaves (*kasuri methi*)

1 tablespoon carom seeds

4 tablespoons vegetable oil

For the topping

2 boiled potatoes, chopped into small pieces

Chilli and Garlic Chutney (*see* page 221)

handful of gram flour noodles (*sev*)

chilli powder, to taste

salt

To make the biscuits, preheat the oven to 180°C (350°F), Gas Mark 4. Line a couple of large baking trays with nonstick baking paper.

Place the flour, semolina, salt, fenugreek leaves and carom seeds in a large bowl and mix together a little. Add the oil and rub it into the dry ingredients. Add a few spoonfuls of water at a time until you have a soft but sticky dough. Leave the dough to rest at room temperature for 30 minutes.

Roll out the dough on a lightly floured surface as thinly as possible. Prick the dough all over with a fork, then, using a 6cm (2½in) round cutter, stamp out as many circles as possible. (If you prefer, you can make the biscuits larger or smaller.) Then re-roll the offcuts and repeat until you have as many circles as possible.

Place the dough circles on the prepared trays (it doesn't matter if they stretch a bit as you move them) and bake for 20–25 minutes until the biscuits are crisp and golden. Transfer to a wire rack.

To assemble, place the biscuits on a serving plate and put a couple of potato pieces on each one. Spoon a little chutney on to the potato pieces and sprinkle the *sev* over the chutney, followed by some salt and chilli powder to taste. Your *papdi chaat* are now ready to serve. You can eat the biscuits on their own, too, or with a variety of cheeses. They can be stored in an airtight container for up to 8 days.

In India, savoury filled pastries such as these tend to be bought from bakeries rather than made in the home. Coriander and fenugreek seeds give the chicken filling a depth of flavour that contrasts beautifully with the light and crisp puff pastry (I use ready-made puff pastry, which makes this snack quick and easy to prepare). Frying the fenugreek seeds in oil brings out their full nutty taste. The coriander seeds are dry-roasted separately first, then lightly crushed to add crunchy hits of flavour.

Coriander chicken parcels

Makes 10

plain flour, for dusting

500g (1lb 2oz) ready-rolled puff pastry

1 egg, beaten

For the filling

2 tablespoons coriander seeds

3 tablespoons vegetable oil

1 tablespoon fenugreek seeds

2 onions, roughly chopped

300g (10½oz) boneless, skinless chicken breasts, cut into 1cm (½in) cubes

2 teaspoons salt

1 teaspoon chilli powder

1 teaspoon ground coriander

2 tablespoons tomato purée

1 teaspoon garam masala

2 tablespoons double cream

In a large pan, dry-roast the coriander seeds for few minutes over a low heat until they start to change colour. Transfer the seeds to a mortar and crush them lightly with the pestle.

Using the same pan in which you dry-roasted the coriander seeds, heat the oil over a medium-low heat and add the fenugreek seeds. Fry for about 1 minute until the seeds start to change colour, then add the onions and cook for about 5 minutes until golden brown. Add the chicken, crushed coriander seeds, salt, chilli powder and ground coriander and mix well. Add the tomato purée and cook for roughly 10 minutes until the chicken is cooked through. Then stir the garam masala and cream into the chicken mixture and take the pan off the heat. Leave to cool.

Preheat the oven to 190°C (375°F), Gas Mark 5. Lightly flour a baking tray.

On a lightly floured surface, roll out the puff pastry into a rectangle measuring roughly 50cm × 25cm (20in × 10in). Keeping one of the longer edges of the rectangle closest to you, divide the pastry horizontally in half, then cut vertically across both halves at 10cm (4in) intervals to produce 10 small rectangles of pastry.

Put 1 heaped tablespoonful of the cooled chicken filling on one side of a pastry rectangle, avoiding the edges, then brush the edges with some beaten egg. Fold the rectangle in half and seal the sides by pressing with a fork. Repeat with the remaining pastry rectangles and filling. Brush the tops of the parcels with beaten egg.

Transfer the parcels to the prepared baking tray and bake them for 35–40 minutes or until golden brown. Serve warm. These pastries are best eaten on the day they are made. The filling will keep, refrigerated, in an airtight container for up to 4 days.

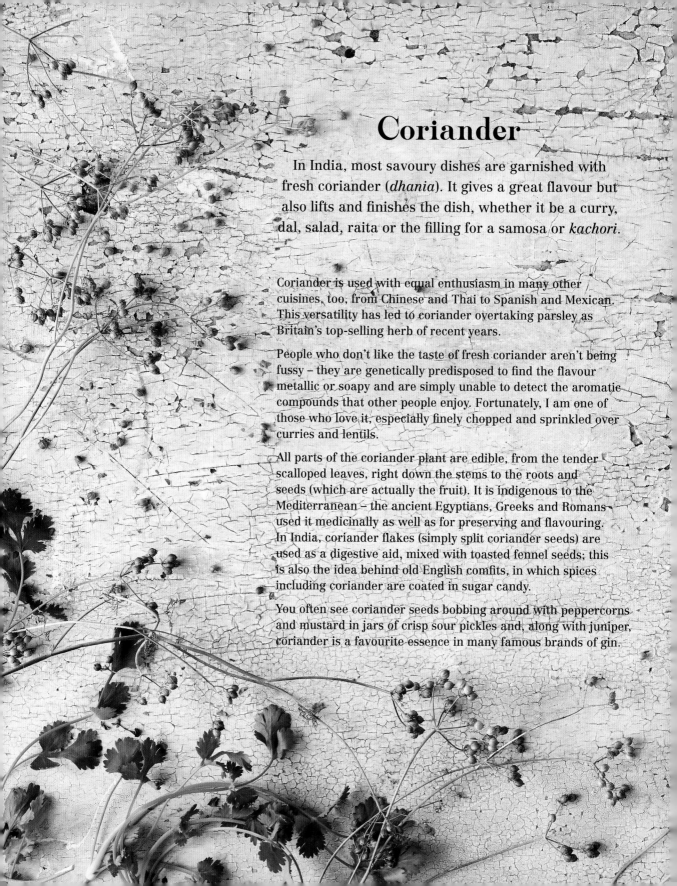

Coriander

In India, most savoury dishes are garnished with fresh coriander (*dhania*). It gives a great flavour but also lifts and finishes the dish, whether it be a curry, dal, salad, raita or the filling for a samosa or *kachori*.

Coriander is used with equal enthusiasm in many other cuisines, too, from Chinese and Thai to Spanish and Mexican. This versatility has led to coriander overtaking parsley as Britain's top-selling herb of recent years.

People who don't like the taste of fresh coriander aren't being fussy – they are genetically predisposed to find the flavour metallic or soapy and are simply unable to detect the aromatic compounds that other people enjoy. Fortunately, I am one of those who love it, especially finely chopped and sprinkled over curries and lentils.

All parts of the coriander plant are edible, from the tender scalloped leaves, right down the stems to the roots and seeds (which are actually the fruit). It is indigenous to the Mediterranean – the ancient Egyptians, Greeks and Romans used it medicinally as well as for preserving and flavouring. In India, coriander flakes (simply split coriander seeds) are used as a digestive aid, mixed with toasted fennel seeds; this is also the idea behind old English comfits, in which spices including coriander are coated in sugar candy.

You often see coriander seeds bobbing around with peppercorns and mustard in jars of crisp sour pickles and, along with juniper, coriander is a favourite essence in many famous brands of gin.

The seeds have a very different flavour to the fresh leaves. When toasted, they exude a lovely burnt orange aroma and have a mild, sweet taste that works with a wide range of ingredients. I particularly like it with lemon, orange and apple, as well as the more savoury cumin and garlic.

Ground coriander is one of the true essentials of Indian cooking – along with salt, chilli powder and turmeric, it is a component of the spice box that every household uses daily. Huge quantities of it go into proprietary curry powder, garam masala and other spice mixes, too.

It is one of the easiest spices to grind with a pestle, so I encourage you to be brave and use toasted and crushed coriander seeds as a seasoning in your everyday cooking. Try it in tomato sauces or soups of carrot or parsnip, for example, or add a pinch to the dough next time you make bread.

Recipes featuring coriander

Light and healthy, these bite-sized snacks make perfect party canapés. Alternatively, use the potato mixture to make larger versions to serve as starters.

Pea and potato cups

Makes 24

For the filling

400g (14oz) frozen peas

800ml (1⅓ pints) boiling water

1 tablespoon vegetable oil

½ teaspoon cumin seeds

½ teaspoon black mustard seeds

½ teaspoon salt

½ teaspoon chilli powder

½ teaspoon garam masala

1 tablespoon lime juice

For the potato cups

butter, for greasing

3 potatoes, boiled, cooled and grated

½ teaspoon salt

½ teaspoon chilli powder

½ teaspoon mango powder (*amchur*)

1 teaspoon cornflour

To make the filling, cook the peas in the measured boiling water for 7–8 minutes. Leave to drain in a sieve for 10 minutes to ensure that there is no water left clinging to the peas.

Heat the oil in a pan set over a low heat, add the cumin and mustard seeds and cook for 1–2 minutes. Once they begin to pop, add the salt, chilli powder and garam masala and cook for 1 minute. Stir in the peas and cook for 2 minutes, then add the lime juice and mix well. Take the pan off the heat and set aside to cool.

Preheat the oven to 200°C (400°F), Gas Mark 6. Grease the recesses of a 24-hole mini cupcake tin.

Put the grated potato into a bowl, add the salt, chilli, mango powder and cornflour and mix to a nice mash. Put 1 tablespoon of the potato mixture into 1 of the recesses of the cupcake tin and press it into a cup shape with your finger, pressing the potato mixture right up to the top so that it lines the entire recess. Repeat with the remaining ingredients. Bake for 20 minutes or until the cups are golden brown.

Transfer the potato cups to a wire rack and leave to cool slightly. Fill with the pea mixture and put them on a serving dish. Serve warm or cold, perhaps with a chutney of your choice. The cups are best eaten on the day they are made. If you have any pea mixture left, it will keep, refrigerated, in an airtight container for up to 3 days. Enjoy it on warm buttery toast.

Tapioca comes to life after you soak it in water and its squidgy texture contrasts beautifully with the crunchy peanuts in these savoury bites. In India, *vada* are a popular tea-time snack and are also enjoyed often when breaking a fast at the end of the day. And, being gluten-free, they are the ideal snack to serve up for those with a gluten intolerance. Serve them with Tamarind and Date Chutney (*see* page 227) and a dollop of natural yogurt.

Tapioca vada

Serves 6–8

200g (7oz) medium tapioca pearls (*sabudana*)

200ml (⅓ pint) water

3 potatoes, boiled and roughly mashed

60g (2¼oz) roasted peanuts, coarsely crushed

juice of 1 lime

2.5cm (1in) piece of fresh root ginger, peeled and grated

1–2 green chillies, finely chopped

2 teaspoons ground cumin

pinch of granulated sugar

1½ teaspoons salt, plus salt flakes to garnish

vegetable oil, for greasing and deep-frying

Wash and drain the tapioca pearls, then soak them in the measured water for 2 hours or until all the water has been absorbed.

In a large mixing bowl, combine the rehydrated tapioca, mashed potato, crushed roasted peanuts, lime juice, ginger, green chillies, cumin, sugar and salt and mix well.

Using oiled palms, shape 1–2 tablespoons of the mixture into a ball and flatten it slightly. Place the disc on a plate. Repeat the shaping process until all the mixture is used.

Pour vegetable oil into a tall saucepan to a depth of one-third (or use a deep-fat fryer and follow the manufacturer's instructions). Heat the oil carefully over a low heat until a breadcrumb sizzles and turns brown when dropped into it. Once it is hot, slide in 5–6 *vada* and fry gently, in batches, for about 2 minutes on each side until brown, turning them with a slotted spoon. Remove from the oil and drain the *vada* on a plate lined with kitchen paper. These are best served hot, sprinkled with salt flakes, and taste best when eaten on the day of cooking.

Buckwheat flour, known as *kuttu* in India, is often eaten at the end of days of fasting. My mother-in-law makes these simple buckwheat pakoras; they taste unlike other pakoras you may have tried, and are absolutely delicious. This is another perfect snack to roll out for someone with a gluten intolerance. Enjoy the pakoras with Cucumber Raita (*see* page 232), or seasoned natural yogurt.

Buckwheat potato pakoras

Serves 4

100g (3½oz) buckwheat flour

½ teaspoon salt

¼ teaspoon chilli powder

1 teaspoon ground cumin

1 teaspoon pomegranate powder (*anardana*)

180ml (6fl oz) water

sunflower oil, for deep-frying

2 potatoes, boiled, cooled and cut into 2.5cm (1in) cubes

Cucumber Raita (*see* page 232), to serve

Combine the buckwheat flour, salt, chilli powder, cumin and pomegranate powder in a bowl. Slowly add the measured water, stirring to make a batter – you might not need all the water or you may need a bit more. You can use a spoon for this, but I prefer to use my hands so that I can feel when the mixture has the right consistency, which should be runny, like pancake batter.

Pour vegetable oil into a heavy saucepan to a depth of one-third (or use a deep-fat fryer and follow the manufacturer's instructions). Heat the oil slowly over a medium heat until a breadcrumb sizzles and turns brown when dropped into it. Once it is hot, dip a few potato pieces into the batter, turning to ensure that they are well coated, then carefully slide them into the hot oil. Fry, in batches, for 2 minutes on each side or until the batter is crisp and thoroughly cooked. Drain on a plate lined with kitchen paper. Serve hot with Cucumber Raita. The pakoras will keep, refrigerated, in an airtight container, for up to 4 days. Warm them in an oven preheated to 180°C (350°F), Gas Mark 4 for 10 minutes before serving.

There is a small café close to my parents' home that makes these crunchy, delicious snacks fresh every morning – my dad always buys them for us for breakfast when we visit. In England, I make pakoras to hand round at parties or barbecues and they are always loved by everyone. The hot oil in the batter makes them nice and crisp and helps the pakoras absorb less oil during frying. Serve with Coriander and Mint Chutney (*see* page 220) or Tamarind and Date Chutney (*see* page 227).

Spinach pakoras

Serves 4–6

200g (7oz) spinach, finely chopped

1 onion, finely chopped

handful of fresh coriander leaves, finely chopped

2 green chillies, finely chopped

2.5cm (1in) piece of fresh root ginger, peeled and finely grated

150g (5¹/₂oz) gram (chickpea) flour

75g (2³/₄oz) rice flour

1 teaspoon salt

vegetable oil, for cooking and deep-frying

5 tablespoons water

Coriander and Mint Chutney (*see* page 220) or Tamarind and Date Chutney (*see* page 227)

Put the spinach, onion, coriander, chillies and ginger in a large bowl and give them a good stir. In a separate bowl, thoroughly combine the gram flour, rice flour and salt. Tip this into the spinach mixture and mix well.

Heat 2 teaspoons vegetable oil in a small pan, then add the hot oil to the spinach mixture along with the measured water. Stir to make a thick batter.

Pour some vegetable oil into a tall saucepan to a depth of one-third (or use a deep-fat fryer and follow the manufacturer's instructions). Heat the oil over a medium heat until a breadcrumb sizzles and turns brown when dropped into it.

Use spoons to help you shape rugged balls of batter that are roughly the size of a lime and gently slide them into the hot oil. Fry them, in batches, for 2–3 minutes on each side until the pakoras are brown and crisp. Drain on a plate lined with kitchen paper. Serve hot with Coriander and Mint Chutney or Tamarind and Date Chutney. The pakoras will keep, refrigerated, in an airtight container for up to 4 days. Warm them in an oven preheated to 180°C (350°F), Gas Mark 4 for 15 minutes before serving.

With sweet, crunchy cashews, creamy paneer and a little zing from fresh green chilli and coriander, these bite-sized balls make irresistible party canapés. They are also wonderful as a starter, served with salad and Coriander and Mint Chutney (*see* page 220). Vegetarian koftas are often made from potatoes, chopped vegetables and lentils, but for this recipe I have chosen cashew nuts, which in India are used in many types of dishes, including curries and desserts. Desiccated coconut helps give the koftas an appealing texture.

Cashew nut and paneer koftas

Serves 6–8

225g (8oz) paneer

2 potatoes, boiled

100g (3^1/$_2$oz) cashew nuts

75g (2^3/$_4$oz) white bread

50g (1^3/$_4$oz) desiccated coconut

handful of fresh coriander leaves, finely chopped

1–2 green chillies, finely chopped

1^1/$_2$ teaspoons salt

vegetable oil, for deep-frying

Coriander and Mint Chutney (*see* page 220) or a raita (*see* pages 232–235), to serve

Grate the paneer and boiled potatoes into a large mixing bowl.

Using a food processor, finely grind the cashew nuts, then add the bread and blitz once more. Mix the pulverized bread and ground nuts into the potato mixture with the desiccated coconut, coriander, chilli and salt. Combine the ingredients well and bring the mixture into a ball. Divide this into bite-sized portions and shape these into balls, compressing them tightly.

Pour vegetable oil into a tall saucepan to a depth of one-third (or use a deep-fat fryer and follow the manufacturer's instructions). Heat the oil over a medium heat until a breadcrumb sizzles and turns brown when dropped into it. Once it is hot, carefully drop some of the koftas into the oil and fry, in batches, for 2 minutes on each side until golden brown. Drain on a plate lined with kitchen paper. Serve hot with Coriander and Mint Chutney or a raita. The koftas will keep, refrigerated, in an airtight container for up to 3 days. Reheat them in an oven preheated to 180°C (350°F), Gas Mark 4 for 10–15 minutes before serving.

Light, crisp and delicious, these little twists make great party food or a cheeky snack at home. The mix of flaky and crumbly pastries is fun and quite addictive, especially with the sweet-and-sour onion chutney running through the middle.

Double pastry twists

Makes 20–22

plain flour, for dusting

325g (11½oz) ready-rolled puff pastry

6 tablespoons Onion Chutney (*see* page 227)

1 egg, beaten

For the shortcrust pastry

300g (10½oz) plain flour

pinch of salt

150g (5½oz) chilled unsalted butter, diced

1 large egg

1 teaspoon lemon juice

2 tablespoons cold water

First make the shortcrust pastry. Put the flour and salt in a large bowl. Add the butter cubes and rub them into the flour with your fingertips until the mixture resembles breadcrumbs. In a small bowl, mix the egg, lemon juice and measured water together. Slowly mix this into the flour mixture to bring the dough together – you might not need all the liquid. Knead the dough for a few seconds. Wrap the pastry in clingfilm and leave it to rest, refrigerated, for 15–20 minutes.

Preheat the oven to 200°C (400°F), Gas Mark 6. Lightly dust 2 baking trays with flour.

Roll out the ready-rolled puff pastry to a rectangle measuring roughly 50cm × 35cm (20in × 14in). Roll out the shortcrust pastry to the same size. Spread the Onion Chutney over the shortcrust pastry, then brush a little beaten egg over the chutney. Lay the puff pastry on top of the shortcrust pastry with the chutney layer in between, like a sandwich.

Trim off the edges of the pastry sandwich to neaten it, then cut it across a longer edge into roughly 20–22 strips that are 2cm (¾in) wide. Twist each strip so that the puff pastry is on the inner curves. Lay the twists on the prepared trays and lightly brush with beaten egg. Bake for 12–15 minutes until golden brown and crispy. Serve warm, or transfer to a wire rack to cool. These pastry twists are best eaten on the day they are made.

Kachoris are a popular Indian street food and are made with all sorts of fillings – fried onions, green peas and chickpeas, to name a few. They are served hot with chutney, yogurt and peas, or cold on their own. In this version they are stuffed with deliciously spiced *urad dal*. Serve them with Tamarind and Date Chutney (*see* page 227).

Dal kachori

Makes 14

For the filling

150g (5¹/₂oz) spilt black lentils (*urad dal*)

600ml (20fl oz) boiling water

¹/₂ teaspoon cumin seeds

¹/₂ teaspoon fennel seeds

2 cloves

2 tablespoons vegetable oil

2 tablespoons gram (chickpea) flour

pinch of asafoetida

2.5cm (1in) piece of fresh root ginger, peeled and finely chopped

¹/₂ teaspoon chilli powder

1 green chilli, finely chopped

¹/₂ teaspoon garam masala

1¹/₂ teaspoons mango powder (*amchur*)

pinch of granulated sugar

salt

For the pastry

200g (7oz) plain flour

¹/₂ teaspoon salt

¹/₂ teaspoon carom seeds

3 tablespoons ghee or vegetable oil, plus extra oil for greasing and deep-frying

about 5 tablespoons water

First prepare the filling. Put the lentils in a saucepan, add the measured boiling water and leave to soak for 15 minutes. Transfer the pan to the hob and cook over a medium heat for 15 minutes. Drain the lentils and set aside.

In a shallow pan, dry-roast the cumin seeds, fennel seeds and cloves for 1–2 minutes or until they start to change colour. Transfer the dry-roasted spices to a mortar and grind them to a fine powder with the pestle. Set aside.

Using the pan in which you dry-roasted the spices, heat the oil over a low heat and add the gram flour. Sauté for 2 minutes, then add the asafoetida, drained lentils, ginger, chilli powder, chopped chilli, garam masala, mango powder, sugar, salt to taste and the ground spices. Mix well, cook for 2 minutes, then set aside to cool.

To make the pastry, mix the flour, salt, carom seeds and ghee or oil together in a bowl. Slowly add the measured water and, using your hands, bring the mixture together into a dough – you might not need all the water, or you may need a little more. Knead the dough on a lightly oiled surface for 5 minutes, then return it to the bowl, cover with a tea towel and leave for 15 minutes.

Roughly divide the dough into 14 portions. Roll out 1 portion into a circle with a diameter of 7.5–10cm (3–4in). Spoon 1–2 tablespoons of the filling mixture into the centre of the circle. Dampen the edges of the dough circle with water, then gather them up in a pleating motion and seal together above the filling. Gently press down on the parcel and roll it a little so that it is quite flat and properly sealed, but take care not to break open the dough to expose the filling. Repeat with the remaining dough and filling.

Pour vegetable oil into a tall saucepan to a depth of one-third (or use a deep-fat fryer and follow the manufacturer's instructions). Heat the oil over a low heat until a breadcrumb sizzles and turns brown when dropped into it. Once it is hot, carefully add 1–2 *kachoris* and cook, in batches, for 2 minutes on each side or until they are golden. Remove from the oil and drain on a plate lined with kitchen paper. Serve warm or cold. The *kachoris* will keep, refrigerated, in an airtight container for up to 4 days. Warm them in a frying pan or in an oven preheated to 180°C (350°F), Gas Mark 4 for 15 minutes before serving.

Semolina is common in Indian cooking – flecked with spices, herbs and dal to make the South Indian breakfast dish *upma*, for instance, or cooked with milk and ghee for fudgy *halwa* pudding, which is loved all over the country. My savoury semolina cake is full of flavour, thanks to all the different vegetables and fresh spices included, and it is very quick and easy to make, too. Using coarse semolina, rather than a finely ground flour, gives the cake an irresistibly crunchy crust. I would serve this with Tomato and Garlic Chutney (*see* page 224).

Savoury semolina cake

Serves 14–16

butter, for greasing

165g (5³/₄oz) coarse semolina

125ml (4fl oz) natural yogurt

125ml (4fl oz) water

1 onion, finely chopped

1 carrot, grated

100g (3¹/₂oz) spinach, roughly chopped

2.5cm (1in) piece of fresh root ginger, peeled and finely grated

2 green chillies, finely chopped

1¹/₄ teaspoons salt

¹/₂ teaspoon ground turmeric

¹/₂ teaspoon bicarbonate of soda

1 egg, beaten

2 tablespoons vegetable oil

1 teaspoon black mustard seeds

Tomato and Garlic Chutney (*see* page 224), to serve

Preheat the oven to 180°C (350°F), Gas Mark 4. Grease a 25cm (10in) round cake tin and line it with nonstick baking paper.

In a large bowl, mix all the ingredients, except for oil and mustard seeds, together well with a wooden spoon.

In a small pan, heat the oil over a medium heat and add the mustard seeds to it. Once they begin to pop, pour the oil and seeds over the cake mixture and mix well with the wooden spoon. Pour the cake mixture into the prepared tin.

Bake for 1 hour or until a skewer inserted into the centre of the cake comes out clean. Leave to cool in the tin for 10 minutes, then turn out on to a wire rack. Serve warm with the Tomato and Garlic Chutney. This savoury cake tastes best on the day it is made.

Breads

Everyone loves freshly baked bread and, for special occasions, a *couronne* (a traditional French 'crown' of bread, filled with sweet or savoury flavours) makes a perfect dinner party centrepiece. In this recipe I use a potato mixture that, in India, is a typical stuffing for parathas or naans, but to add the wow factor, I include Chilli and Garlic Chutney. If you or your guests would prefer something less fiery, simply substitute a milder chutney (*see* pages 220–227 for chutney recipes).

Savoury potato couronne

Serves 8–10

250g (9oz) strong white bread flour, plus extra for dusting

5g (¹⁄₈oz) salt

8g (¹⁄₄oz) fast-action dried yeast

50g (1³⁄₄oz) unsalted butter, softened

1 egg, lightly beaten

135ml (4¹⁄₂fl oz) warm milk

oil, for greasing

400g (14oz) potatoes

¹⁄₂ teaspoon salt

¹⁄₄ teaspoon mango powder (*amchur*)

2 handfuls of fresh coriander leaves, finely chopped

2 tablespoons Chilli and Garlic Chutney (*see* page 221)

Mix the flour, salt and yeast together in a bowl. Add the butter, egg and milk and mix well. Knead the dough by hand on a lightly floured surface for 8–10 minutes until you have a soft dough (or use a stand mixer fitted with a dough hook). Put the dough in a lightly oiled bowl, cover the bowl with clingfilm and leave the dough to rise for 1 hour or until doubled in size.

Boil the potatoes for 20 minutes or until cooked. When cool enough to handle, grate them into a mixing bowl. Add the salt, mango powder and chopped coriander. Mix well, cover and set aside.

Once the dough is ready, roll it out on a lightly floured surface into a rectangle roughly measuring 50cm × 38cm (20in × 15in). Keeping one of the long edges near you (parallel to the edge of the work surface), spread the chutney evenly over the dough. On top of this, evenly spread the potato mixture. Roll up the dough, like a Swiss roll, from the long edge nearest to you. Then cut it in half lengthways, leaving the 2 lengths just joined at one end. Twist the 2 dough lengths together around each other, then bring the twist together in a circle and join the loose ends. Transfer to a lightly floured baking tray. Put the tray in a clean plastic bag and leave to prove for 1 hour or until doubled in size.

Preheat the oven to 200°C (400°F), Gas Mark 6.

Bake the couronne for 35–40 minutes. Leave it to rest for 15 minutes, then serve. This is best eaten on the day it is made. If you have some left over, leave it covered in a cool place and consume it by the end of the next day.

This is one of those quick breads, rather like a savoury cake. Indians love the combination of cheese and tomato just as much as the Brits and Italians! A hint of bitter *kasuri methi* (dried fenugreek leaves) goes well with the mild, creamy paneer and the sweet fresh tomato. I couldn't resist including some green chilli and coriander. Serve the loaf warm or cold with Coriander and Mint Chutney (*see* page 220) or Red Pepper and Almond Chutney (*see* page 225).

Tomato and paneer loaf

Serves 6–8

200g (7oz) self-raising flour

1 teaspoon salt

1 teaspoon baking powder

1/2 teaspoon bicarbonate of soda

1 tablespoon dried fenugreek leaves (*kasuri methi*)

1 tomato, finely chopped

2 large eggs

100ml (3¹/₂fl oz) vegetable oil, plus extra for greasing

100ml (3¹/₂fl oz) natural yogurt

100g (3¹/₂oz) paneer, grated

1 green chilli, finely chopped

handful of fresh coriander leaves, finely chopped

Preheat the oven to 180°C (350°F), Gas Mark 4. Grease a 900g (2lb) loaf tin.

Put the flour, salt, baking powder, bicarbonate of soda and *kasuri methi* in a large bowl.

In a jug, combine the tomato, eggs, oil, yogurt, paneer, chilli and chopped coriander and mix well.

Pour the contents of the jug into the dry ingredients and quickly stir the mixture into a batter. Pour the mixture into the prepared loaf tin and bake for 40–45 minutes or until a skewer inserted into the centre of the loaf comes out clean. Leave to cool in the tin for 10 minutes, then serve. Well wrapped in kitchen foil or in an airtight container, this bread will keep for up to 2 days.

Use these simple rolls to add extra flavour to burgers. They go very well with soups and curries, too. The onions are cooked lightly to bring out their sweetness, which enhances the nutty taste of the pine nuts. Serve the rolls warm or cold with Chilli and Garlic Chutney (*see* page 221).

Pine nut and onion rolls

Makes 12

300g (10½oz) strong white bread flour, plus extra for dusting

200g (7oz) seeded wholemeal bread flour

10g (⅓oz) salt

10g (⅓oz) fast-action dried yeast

250ml (9fl oz) water

100ml (3½fl oz) milk

1 tablespoon olive oil, plus extra for greasing

1 large onion, finely chopped

2 tablespoons pine nuts

2 tablespoons nigella seeds (*kalonji*)

Chilli and Garlic Chutney (*see* page 221), to serve

Tip the flours into a large mixing bowl. Add the salt and yeast at opposite sides of the bowl. Combine the measured water and milk in a jug and slowly add this to the flour, mixing to form a dough – you might not need all the liquid or you may need a bit more. Knead the dough on a lightly oiled surface for 8–10 minutes until smooth (or use a stand mixer fitted with a dough hook). Put the dough in a lightly oiled bowl, cover with clingfilm and leave to rise for 1 hour or until doubled in size.

While the dough is rising, prepare the onion. Heat the oil in a saucepan, add the onion and cook over a low heat until light golden, then take the pan off the heat. In a dry frying pan, toast the pine nuts for a couple of minutes, stirring to prevent scorching. When fragrant and golden, tip the pine nuts in with the cooked onion and stir well. Set aside to cool.

Once the dough has doubled in size, knock out the air on a lightly oiled surface. Add the onion mixture and knead well to ensure that the mixture is evenly distributed throughout the dough.

Divide the dough into 12 equal portions and roll them on your work surface with the palm of your hand to give them a nice round shape. Lightly brush some water on the buns and sprinkle a few nigella seeds on top.

Line 2 baking trays with nonstick baking paper. Sprinkle with flour and place the prepared rolls on top, keeping them well spaced. Put each tray in a lightly oiled plastic bag and leave the buns to prove for 1 hour or until doubled in size.

Preheat the oven to 220°C (425°F), Gas Mark 7. Put a roasting tray filled with water on the bottom shelf of the oven to create steam.

Once the buns have proved, remove the plastic bags and bake the rolls for 20–25 minutes or until they sound hollow when tapped on the bases. Transfer to a wire rack and leave to cool. Serve with Chilli and Garlic Chutney. Well wrapped in kitchen foil, these rolls will keep for up to 3 days.

Carom

When I was young, if my sisters or I were unwell or didn't feel like eating, my mother would produce a deliciously crispy and salty ghee and carom seed paratha within minutes. Carom (also known as *ajwain* and *ajowan*) is thought to assist many ailments, from sore throats to indigestion, and is a common ingredient in household remedies in India.

The striped grey-green carom seeds look like a smaller version of cumin or caraway seeds, to which carom is related. However, the assertive flavour is usually compared to thyme or oregano, with the bonus of a tingling, warm peppery aftertaste. Carom is harsh and bitter eaten raw; cooking mellows the sharpness and highlights carom's complexity. Its uses are almost always savoury, yet carom is versatile: try it in breads, crackers, pastries, deep-fried batters and pickles for lovely flavour and depth.

I (along with the rest of India) tend not to use ground or powdered carom and think it best to buy whole seeds. If a recipe asks for ground carom, toast it first in a preheated heavy-based frying pan. Tip the toasted seeds into a mortar and let them cool, then crush or grind them with a pestle.

Carom loves starchy foods, everything from root vegetables and potatoes to beans, lentils, rice and anything made with flour. A few carom seeds are a wonderful addition to *tarka* (*tadka*) *dal*.

I love the lingering tang it gives to plain pastry in pastry parcels. Its thyme-like flavour is perfect with onions and tomatoes; a dash in onion pakora batter enhances the aroma and maximizes the pakoras' digestibility. Or add a tiny pinch in place of thyme or oregano to soups and sauces. The seed's antiseptic and preservative qualities make it an ideal inclusion for pickles and chutneys. When the herbal notes of carom meet the sweet-sour zing of tamarind, it is a delicious marriage – try this combination in marinades.

Pitta is simple to make and it's perfect for sandwiches, picnics and barbecues. My version includes carom seeds and fresh coriander. I like to fill these with potato tikki, a popular Indian tea-time snack. Serve with Indian Coleslaw (*see* page 232), Chilli and Garlic Chutney (*see* page 221) or Tomato and Garlic Chutney (*see* page 224).

Carom seed pitta with potato tikki

Serves 3–4

For the pitta bread

250g (9oz) strong white bread flour, plus extra for dusting

5g (1/8oz) salt

7g (1/5oz) sachet fast-action dried yeast

1 teaspoon carom seeds

2 tablespoons finely chopped fresh coriander leaves

1 tablespoon olive oil, plus extra for greasing

about 160ml (5 1/2 fl oz) water

semolina, for dusting

For the potato tikki

3 potatoes, boiled, peeled and mashed

1 carrot, grated

2 slices of white bread, made into breadcrumbs

1/2 teaspoon salt

1/2 teaspoon chilli powder

1/2 teaspoon mango powder

1/2 teaspoon garam masala

1 green chilli, finely chopped

300g (10 1/2 oz) black poppy seeds

vegetable oil, for shallow-frying

To serve

Indian Coleslaw (*see* page 232)

Chilli and Garlic Chutney (*see* page 221) or Tomato and Garlic Chutney (*see* page 224)

To make the pittas, combine the flour, salt, yeast, carom seeds, coriander and olive oil in a large bowl and mix well. Slowly stir in the measured water to form a dough – you might not need all the measured water or you may need a bit more. On a lightly oiled surface, knead the dough for 8–10 minutes until soft and smooth (or use a stand mixer fitted with a dough hook). Put the dough in a lightly oiled bowl, cover the bowl with clingfilm and leave to rise for 1 hour or until doubled in size. (This is a good time in which to boil the potatoes and prepare the breadcrumbs, ready to make the potato tikki.)

To bake the pittas, preheat the oven to 220°C (425°F), Gas Mark 7. Put 2 baking trays in the oven to heat up.

Lightly dust your work surface with flour and semolina. Tip the risen dough on to the surface and fold it inwards to knock out all the air. Divide the dough into 6–8 portions and roll each into an oval that is roughly 15cm (6in) long and 3mm (1/8in) thick. Lay the rolled pittas on the hot baking trays and bake for 8–10 minutes, just until they puff up and start to get a bit of colour. Set aside to cool.

To make the potato tikki, combine all the ingredients, except the poppy seeds and vegetable oil, in a bowl and mix well. Divide the mixture into 8–10 portions, roll these into balls and coat them generously in the poppy seeds. Press down lightly to make flat oval shapes.

In a wide pan, heat some vegetable oil for shallow-frying over a medium heat. Once hot, fry the potato tikki for 2 minutes on each side or until brown and crispy. Serve the tikki inside the pitta bread, portioning them to your liking, adding some Indian Coleslaw and chutney. The pitta and tikki are best eaten within 24 hours of making.

Sabjis (or *subzis*) are simple spiced vegetable dishes, made to serve with bread or rice. They are popular throughout India. The twist in this recipe is that I'm not serving the *sabji* with naan, chapatti or roti, but with a European-style white loaf flavoured with cumin and curry powder.

Cumin bread with smoked aubergine

Serves 8–10

For the bread

500g (1lb 2oz) strong white bread flour, plus extra for dusting

10g (⅓oz) salt

10g (⅓oz) fast-action dried yeast

35g (1¼oz) unsalted butter, softened

1 tablespoon curry powder

1 teaspoon cumin seeds

about 325ml (11fl oz) water

oil, for greasing

For the smoked aubergine *sabji*

1 aubergine

2 tablespoons vegetable oil, plus extra for brushing

1 teaspoon black mustard seeds

2 onions, finely chopped

2 garlic cloves, finely chopped

2.5cm (1in) piece of fresh root ginger, peeled and finely chopped

2 tomatoes, finely chopped

1 teaspoon salt

½ teaspoon chilli powder

handful of fresh coriander leaves, finely chopped

In a large bowl, mix the flour, salt, yeast, butter, curry powder and cumin seeds together. Slowly add the measured water to bring the mixture together into a dough – you might not need all the water or you may need a bit more. Knead the dough on a lightly floured surface for 8–10 minutes until smooth (or use a stand mixer fitted with a dough hook). Put it into a lightly oiled bowl and cover it with clingfilm. Leave to rise for 1 hour or until doubled in size.

On a lightly floured surface, knock out all the air from the dough. Fold the edge of the dough inwards several times, then shape the dough into a smooth ball. Leave it on a lightly floured baking tray and place the tray in a lightly oiled plastic bag. Leave to prove for 1 hour or until doubled in size.

Preheat the oven to 200°C (400°F), Gas Mark 6. Bake the bread for 30–35 minutes or until golden brown and the loaf sounds hollow when tapped underneath. Leave it on a wire rack to cool for 10 minutes before serving.

To prepare the smoked aubergine *sabji*, preheat the grill on a high setting. Brush some oil on the aubergine and prick it all over with a fork. Grill for 20–25 minutes, turning it often. Leave the grilled aubergine to cool for 10 minutes, then peel off the charred skin and chop the aubergine flesh into small pieces.

In a saucepan, heat the oil over a medium-low heat and add the mustard seeds. Once they begin to pop, add the onions and cook until slightly softened. Add the garlic and ginger and cook for a further 2 minutes. Now add the tomatoes and cook over a medium heat for 5 minutes. Add the chopped aubergine, salt and chilli powder to the pan and mix well. Cover and cook for 10–15 minutes until everything is well mixed. Sprinkle the chopped coriander on top and serve with the cumin bread. The aubergine *sabji* will keep, refrigerated, in an airtight container for up to 4 days. Reheat it in a saucepan or microwave oven before serving. Well wrapped in kitchen foil, the bread will keep for 2–3 days.

Cumin

Known as *jeera* in Hindi, cumin is an essential component of the household spice box and a key ingredient in many spice blends, including garam masala. India is the world's largest producer and consumer of cumin, although the spice probably originated in Egypt or the Eastern Mediterranean.

There are two varieties of cumin, or three if you include the fact that *kalonji* or nigella seeds are often called black cumin, even though they are not related. Here I am referring to true cumins of the *Apiaceae* plant family. The seeds are striped and crescent shaped, the black seeds slightly smaller, sweeter and more delicate in flavour than the common light brown variety. In India, black cumin is especially used in rice dishes.

The flavour of cumin is strong and distinctive. It has a touch of sweetness and brings a woody note to dishes, but is too harsh when eaten raw. It really should be dry-roasted or fried in oil before use so that it mellows and releases its nutty, lemony fragrance. Fried whole cumin seeds will lift any lentil dish or curry, meat or vegetable curry, soup or rice dish. They are particularly good mixed with onions and tomatoes, or try them in bread dough with a little chopped fresh coriander. Unlike the plumper spices, there is no need to crush cumin seeds after frying or toasting and they look very attractive strewn over food.

Ground cumin is terrific in marinades for all sorts of meat and veg, and works very well with new potatoes, mashed potatoes and fillings for pastry parcels. It is a staple in raitas, where it is often the only spice used besides salt, and gives a refreshing, lemony kick to the yogurt base.

Coriander is cumin's best friend, the two forming the backbone of garam masala and commercial curry powders.

Recipes featuring cumin

Most Indian families keep coriander-mint chutney to hand in the refrigerator – it's a staple. In this loaf, I add layers of this well-loved chutney in the dough, along with a sprinkling of Kashmiri chilli. There's also some turmeric in the bread, to add a warming flavour and colour. The result makes a vibrant centrepiece for any table.

Coriander and mint loaf

Serves 10–12

500g (1lb 2oz) strong white bread flour, plus extra for dusting

10g (⅓oz) fast-action dried yeast

10g (⅓oz) salt

1 teaspoon ground turmeric

30g (1oz) unsalted butter, softened

about 325ml (11fl oz) milk

oil, for greasing

6–8 tablespoons Coriander and Mint Chutney (*see* page 220)

1 teaspoon Kashmiri chilli powder

In a large bowl, combine the flour, yeast, salt, turmeric and butter. Slowly stir in the milk – you might not need all the milk or you may need a bit more. Bring the mixture together into a dough. Knead on a lightly oiled surface for 8–10 minutes (or use a stand mixer fitted with a dough hook). Put the dough in a lightly oiled bowl, cover the bowl with clingfilm and leave the dough to rise for 1 hour or until doubled in size.

When ready, roll out the dough on a lightly floured surface into a square roughly 37–38cm (14½–15in) wide. Spread the chutney evenly over the top of the dough and sprinkle with the chilli powder.

Roll up the dough from one side, like a Swiss roll, ensuring that the roll is nice and tight. Use a sharp knife to cut it into 13–14 pieces. Lightly flour a baking tray. Stand the slices of dough on the prepared tray in a loaf shape, overlapping them to widen the loaf and create an attractive the pattern. Put the tray in a well-oiled plastic bag and leave the dough to prove for 1 hour or until doubled in size.

Heat the oven to 200°C (400°F), Gas Mark 6. Bake for 30–35 minutes or until the bread sounds hollow when tapped on the base. Transfer to a wire rack and leave to cool. Well wrapped in kitchen foil, this bread will keep for up to 3 days.

This super-light loaf is packed with flavours – earthy spinach, warming cumin and chilli, zingy lime juice plus toasty pine nuts. Even so, it is very quick to make and I think you'll turn to this recipe again and again. Enjoy the loaf plain or toasted, spread with butter or chutney. You can take it on picnics, serve it alongside light summer meals or cut it into small squares and top with onion chutney for a speedy party nibble.

Spinach and spice loaf

Serves 10

butter, for greasing
100g (3½oz) spinach
100ml (3½fl oz) boiling water
2 large eggs
120ml (4fl oz) garlic-and-herb-infused rapeseed or sunflower oil
2 garlic cloves, finely chopped
180ml (6¼fl oz) natural yogurt
1 tablespoon lime juice
220g (7¾oz) self-raising flour
50g (1¾oz) pine nuts
1 teaspoon baking powder
½ teaspoon bicarbonate of soda
½ teaspoon chilli flakes
½ teaspoon ground cumin

Preheat the oven to 180°C (350°F), Gas Mark 4. Grease a 900g (2lb) loaf tin and line it with nonstick baking paper.

Put the spinach in a saucepan and cover it with the measured boiling water. Cover with a lid and cook over a low heat for 3–4 minutes. Drain the spinach thoroughly and, once it is cool enough to handle, squeeze out the excess water.

In a bowl, combine the eggs, oil, garlic, yogurt and lime juice and whisk well.

Put the flour, pine nuts, baking powder, bicarbonate of soda, chilli flakes and cumin into a separate bowl and mix well. Tip this into the egg mixture and fold it in until the ingredients are evenly combined. Spoon the mixture into the prepared tin and bake for 25–30 minutes until a skewer inserted into the centre of the loaf comes out clean. Leave to cool in the tin for 10 minutes, then remove the loaf from the tin and eat warm or cold. This loaf will keep in an airtight container for up to 3 days.

This beautiful loaf has the indulgent feel of a cake yet is, in fact, very light. I love eating it warm, or just toasted with some butter, but it is also utterly delicious used for sandwiches, whether sweet or savoury. The cocoa creates a deep-coloured loaf, while the chilli provides a real kick to the aftertaste.

Chocolate and chilli loaf

Serves 8–10

400g (14oz) strong white bread flour, plus extra for dusting

25g (1oz) cocoa powder

5g ($^1/_8$oz) salt

8g ($^1/_4$oz) fast-action dried yeast

25g (1oz) light soft brown sugar

1 teaspoon chilli flakes

1 tablespoon olive oil, plus extra for greasing

about 300ml ($^1/_2$ pint) water

In a large bowl, mix the flour, cocoa powder, salt, yeast, sugar, chilli flakes and olive oil together. Slowly add just enough of the measured water to bring the mixture together into a dough – you might not need all the water or you may need a bit more. Knead the dough on a lightly floured surface for 8–10 minutes or until smooth (or use a stand mixer fitted with a dough hook). Then put the dough in a lightly oiled bowl and cover the bowl with clingfilm. Leave to rise for 1 hour or until doubled in size.

Once the dough has risen, knock it back on a lightly floured surface. Fold the edge of the dough inwards several times, then shape the dough into a cylinder. Place this in a lightly floured 900g (2lb) loaf tin. Cover the tin with an oiled plastic bag and leave the dough to prove for 1 hour or until doubled in size.

Preheat the oven to 200°C (400°F), Gas Mark 6.

Bake for 30–35 minutes or until the loaf sounds hollow when tapped on the base. Once baked, remove the bread from the tin and leave to cool on a wire rack. Well wrapped in kitchen foil, this bread will keep for up to 3 days.

The chocolate and walnut loaf I made on the TV programme *The Great British Bake Off* was such a hit with everyone who tasted it, I was keen to take it a step further and add an Indian twist to the recipe. This simple but stunning loaf is the result, which proves popular with adults and children alike. The combination of flavours may be unusual, but they balance each other well.

Star anise, date and chocolate bread

Serves 8–10

For the dough

300g (10½oz) strong white bread flour, plus extra for dusting

10g (⅓oz) fast-action dried yeast

5g (⅛oz) salt

60g (2¼oz) unsalted butter, softened, plus extra for greasing

160ml (5½fl oz) milk

1 large egg, beaten

oil, for greasing

1 egg white, lightly beaten

For the filling

100g (3½oz) milk chocolate

100g (3½oz) plain dark chocolate (minimum 70 per cent cocoa solids)

100g (3½oz) finely ground walnuts

100g (3½oz) pitted dates, finely chopped

100g (3½oz) dark muscovado sugar

100ml (3½fl oz) milk

½ teaspoon ground cinnamon

½ teaspoon ground star anise

For the dough, put the flour, yeast, salt and butter in a large bowl. Mix the milk and whole egg together in a jug and slowly pour this into the flour mixture to bring it together into a dough – you might not need all the liquid or you may need a bit more. Knead the dough on a lightly dusted work surface for 8–10 minutes until soft and smooth (or use a stand mixer fitted with a dough hook). Put it in a lightly oiled bowl, cover the bowl with clingfilm and leave to rise for 1 hour or until doubled in size.

When the dough has almost risen, make the filling. Break both the chocolates into a heatproof bowl and set it over a pan of steaming water until the chocolate has melted, ensuring that the base of the bowl doesn't touch the water beneath it. Once melted, remove from the heat, add the remaining filling ingredients and mix well.

Grease a 900g (2lb) loaf tin with butter. Roll out the dough into a rectangle that is roughly 55cm × 40cm (21½in × 16in). Spread the chocolate filling evenly over it. Tightly roll up the dough from a long edge, like a Swiss roll.

Carefully lift your cylinder of dough and place one end into one corner of the prepared loaf tin. Ease the cylinder into the base of the tin and turn it around on itself at the other end of the tin to form a long U shape. Continue easing the dough cylinder into the tin to form another layer until you reach the end of the dough. Place the tin in an oiled plastic bag and leave to prove for 1 hour.

Preheat the oven to 180°C (350°F), Gas Mark 4.

Brush the risen loaf with the beaten egg white. Bake for 15 minutes, then reduce the oven temperature to 160°C (325°F), Gas Mark 3 and bake for 45 minutes. Leave to cool in the tin for 30 minutes. Enjoy warm or cold. Well wrapped in kitchen foil, this loaf will keep for up to 4 days.

I love making challah – it is so rich yet so light, and, with lemon pickle running through the middle, it is utterly delicious. To match it, I suggest a creamy paneer dish I learned from my mum. The sweet coconut and nutty-tasting curry leaves complement the fresh cheese and, when teamed with the bite of pickle-filled bread, each mouthful is truly amazing.

Lemon challah with coconut paneer

Serves 8–10

For the challah

500g (1lb 2oz) strong white bread flour, plus extra for dusting

10g (⅓oz) salt

10g (⅓oz) fast-action dried yeast

20g (¾oz) caster sugar

2 large eggs, lightly beaten

50ml (2fl oz) warm milk

25g (1oz) unsalted butter, softened

about 180ml (6¼fl oz) water

oil, for greasing

8 heaped tablespoons lemon pickle (available in Asian grocery stores)

1 egg, lightly beaten

To make the challah, combine the flour, salt, yeast and sugar in a large bowl. Add the eggs, milk and butter and mix well, then slowly stir in the measured water to bring the mixture together to form a dough – you might not need all the water or you may need a bit more. On a lightly floured surface, knead the dough for 8–10 minutes (or use a stand mixer fitted with a dough hook). Put the dough in a lightly oiled bowl, cover with clingfilm and leave to rise for 1 hour or until doubled in size.

Line a baking tray with nonstick baking paper. Tip the risen dough on to a lightly floured work surface and knock out the air by folding the dough inwards from the edge. Divide it into 4 equal pieces. Roll out 1 portion into a rectangle measuring 35cm × 10cm (14in × 4in). Spread 2 tablespoons of the pickle lengthways along the middle of the rectangle. Roll it into a big sausage shape. Repeat with the remaining dough and lemon pickle.

Lay the 4 dough cylinders on the prepared tray across each other in 2 pairs of parallel lines in a hashtag shape, with 1 pair running horizontally and 1 pair running vertically. In the corners of the central square of the hashtag (the points where the dough cylinders cross), each cylinder touches another twice – ensure that it is woven underneath the other cylinder at one point, and over the other at the next point.

To weave the hashtag into a circle, you need to weave together the 4 parallel pairs of cylinders that extend from the central circle of the hashtag. Working clockwise around the hashtag shape, take the cylinder that emerges from the corner of the central square from underneath the junction, and wrap it over its parallel cylinder.

When you have completed 1 clockwise rotation, make 1 anticlockwise rotation. This time, take each cylinder to the left of each pair (emerging from underneath the previous junction) and pass it over the cylinder to the left (the right-hand cylinder from the adjacent pair). Tuck in the ends of the cylinders under the challah to make a beautiful circle shape. Carefully put the challah in a plastic bag and leave to prove for 1 hour or until doubled in size.

For the coconut paneer

2 tablespoons vegetable oil

1 tablespoon split black lentils
(*urad dal*)

1 tablespoon black mustard seeds

8 curry leaves

2 red dried chillies

3 onions, thinly sliced

2.5cm (1in) piece of fresh root
ginger, peeled and finely grated

3 garlic cloves, finely grated

2 tomatoes, grated

1 teaspoon salt

$1/2$ teaspoon chilli powder

1 teaspoon ground coriander

$1/2$ teaspoon ground turmeric

1 teaspoon sambhar powder
(a South Indian spice mix available
in Asian grocery stores)

250ml (9fl oz) coconut milk

260g (9$1/2$oz) paneer, cubed

Preheat the oven to 200°C (400°F), Gas Mark 6. Brush the loaf with beaten egg and bake for 20–25 minutes. If it browns very quickly, cover with kitchen foil to avoid burning.

To make the coconut paneer, heat the oil in a saucepan set over a low heat. Add the split lentils, mustard seeds, curry leaves and dried red chillies. Once the mustard seeds start to pop, add the onions and cook until lightly golden. Add the ginger and garlic and cook for 1 minute, then add the grated tomatoes and cook for 2–3 minutes. Stir in the salt, chilli powder, coriander, turmeric and sambhar and mix well. Tip in the coconut milk and cook for 2 minutes. Add the paneer, mix well and cook for a final 2 minutes to allow the flavours to come together. Serve the coconut paneer with the bread. The paneer will keep, refrigerated, in an airtight container for up to 4 days. Well wrapped in kitchen foil, the bread will keep for up to 3 days.

I love the flavour of fried onions sprinkled over biryani. The same idea is applied to bread in this recipe. I add *amchur* (mango powder) and garam masala to the fried onion for extra dimensions of sweetness and aroma. The dough features fennel seeds as well as Kashmiri chilli powder, which is comparatively mild and gives the bread a lovely colour.

Onion and fennel bread

Serves 8–10

For the dough

400g (14oz) strong white bread flour, plus extra for dusting

7g (1/5oz) salt

7g (1/5oz) sachet fast-action dried yeast

1 tablespoon fennel seeds

1 teaspoon Kashmiri chilli powder

25g (1oz) unsalted butter, softened

about 250ml (9fl oz) water

olive oil, for greasing

For the filling

50ml (2fl oz) olive oil

6 onions, thinly sliced

1 teaspoon garam masala

1 teaspoon mango powder (*amchur*)

1/2 teaspoon salt

Tip the flour into a large mixing bowl. Add the salt and yeast at opposite sides of the bowl. Now add the fennel seeds, chilli powder and butter. Slowly add just enough of the measured water to bring the dough together – you might not need all the water or you may need a bit more. Knead the dough on a lightly oiled surface for 8–10 minutes until smooth (or use a stand mixer fitted with a dough hook). Put the dough in a lightly oiled bowl, cover the bowl with clingfilm and leave to rise for at least 1 hour or until doubled in size.

Meanwhile, prepare the filling. Heat the oil in a saucepan set over a low heat, add the onions and cook, stirring occasionally, for 15 minutes or more until the onions are golden brown. Add the garam masala, *amchur* and salt. Mix well, then take the pan off the heat and set aside to cool.

Once the dough has risen, knock it back on a lightly floured surface. Roll it out into a 35–40cm (14–16in) square, then spread the cooled onion mixture over it. Now roll up the square, like a Swiss roll. Cut the roll in half vertically so that you have 2 cylinders, each about 17–20cm (6½–8in) long. Twist the 2 cylinders of dough together like a rope, then coil the length into a circle. Place this on a floured baking tray. Put the tray in an oiled plastic bag and leave the dough to prove for 1 hour or until doubled in size.

Preheat the oven to 200°C (400°F), Gas Mark 6. Bake for 30–35 minutes or until the loaf sounds hollow when tapped on the base. Leave to cool for 10 minutes, then serve. Well wrapped in kitchen foil, this bread will keep for up to 3 days.

Breadsticks are a great snack for a party or any get-together, and an ideal healthy snack for kids after school. The best part is that they go with a variety of dips and chutneys. These breadsticks are made with garlic, which is roasted to bring out its sweetness. The nigella seeds (*kalonji*) add even more flavour. These go well with Onion Chutney (*see* page 227) or Tomato and Garlic Chutney (*see* page 224).

Roasted garlic and kalonji breadsticks

Makes 15

For the roasted garlic

2 tablespoons olive oil, plus extra for greasing

10–15 garlic cloves (unpeeled)

$1/2$ teaspoon salt

$1/2$ teaspoon granulated sugar

1 tablespoon olive oil

For the dough

400g (14oz) strong white bread flour, plus extra for dusting

50g (1¾oz) semolina

8g (¼oz) fast-action dried yeast

8g (¼oz) salt

1 tablespoon nigella seeds (*kalonji*)

about 300ml (½ pint) warm water

First, roast the garlic. Preheat the oven to 200°C (400°F), Gas Mark 6. Put the garlic cloves in a roasting dish with their skins on. Sprinkle with the salt, sugar and olive oil. Roast for 20–25 minutes until golden brown and soft to the touch. Set aside to cool, then remove the skins.

Put the flour, semolina, yeast, salt, nigella seeds (*kalonji*) and olive oil in a large mixing bowl. Slowly mix in the measured warm water to make a soft, sticky dough – you might not need all the water or may need a bit more. Place the dough on a lightly floured work surface and knead it for 8–10 minutes (or knead it in a stand mixer fitted with a dough hook).

Once the dough is stretchy and soft, add the roasted garlic cloves. Knead it for a further 5 minutes until the garlic is well incorporated. Put the dough in a lightly oiled bowl, cover with clingfilm and leave to rise for 1 hour or until doubled in size.

Line 2–3 baking trays with nonstick baking paper and dust them with flour. Tip out the dough on to a lightly floured surface and divide it into 15 equal portions. Stretch each portion into a 20–25cm (8–10in) long strip and place it on a prepared tray. (You can also try shaping the dough in different forms and sizes.) Cover the strips with oiled plastic bags and leave to prove for about 30 minutes.

Heat the oven to 200°C (400°F), Gas Mark 6. Bake the dough strips for 15–20 minutes or until brown and crispy. Transfer to a wire rack and leave to cool. These breadsticks will keep in an airtight container in a cool, dry place for up to 3 days.

Kidney beans are a great favourite in Indian cuisine, although they are not normally used in this manner. These simple flatbreads are terrific served hot with butter and Cucumber Raita (*see* page 232) or Coriander and Mint Chutney (*see* page 220), or alongside a chicken curry or sag paneer.

Rajma paratha

Makes 12

200g (7oz) chapatti flour, plus extra for dusting

100g (3¹/₂oz) plain flour

1¹/₂ teaspoons salt

2 green chillies, finely chopped

handful of fresh coriander leaves, finely chopped

400g (14oz) can red kidney beans, drained

1 tablespoon vegetable oil, plus extra for brushing and cooking

about 200ml (¹/₃ pint) water

Cucumber Raita (*see* page 232) or Coriander and Mint Chutney (*see* page 220), to serve

In a large bowl, combine the chapatti flour and plain flour, then add the salt, chillies and coriander.

Rinse the kidney beans and mash them with your fingers or a fork, keeping a bit of texture. Add the mashed beans to the flour, then add the oil. Gradually incorporate the measured water, mixing to bring the dough together – you might not need all the water or you may need a bit more.

Knead the dough on a lightly floured work surface for 5 minutes. Put it in a clean bowl and cover the bowl with clingfilm. Leave to rest at room temperature for 1 hour.

Divide the dough into 12 equal portions. Roll out 1 portion at a time into a circle roughly measuring 12–15cm (4¹/₂–6in). Brush 1 teaspoon oil over the dough. Fold it in half to make a semicircle, then fold it in half again, making a triangle. Roll this out again into a triangle with sides each measuring 15–18cm (6–7in).

Cook each paratha on a hot griddle or cast-iron frying pan for a couple of minutes on each side, then spread ¹/₂ teaspoon oil over 1 side, cook again, then repeat on the other side. Serve hot. The dough will keep, refrigerated, in an airtight container for up to 3 days. Cook the parathas fresh when you need them and serve with Cucumber Raita or Coriander and Mint Chutney.

Flatbreads, of which parathas are just one variety, are an important part of Indian meals. There are many types of parathas, such as plain, stuffed, flavoured and *lachha* (multilayered), made in different ways. For convenience, it's a good idea to make up a batch of dough and keep it refrigerated, ready for you to roll and cook fresh parathas when you're preparing a meal. In this recipe, I include lentils and fresh herbs in the dough and cook the parathas in butter for extra crispness and flavour. They are lovely enjoyed hot, with extra butter spread over them, and also go well with pickles and chutneys, such as Chilli and Garlic Chutney (*see* page 221). Kids love them with tomato ketchup.

Moong dal paratha

Makes 12

For the dal

200g (7oz) yellow split lentils (*moong dal*)

1 teaspoon salt

1/2 teaspoon ground turmeric

600ml (20fl oz) water

For the dough

300g (10½oz) chapatti flour

1/2 teaspoon salt

1/4 teaspoon ground turmeric

2 green chillies, finely chopped

handful of fresh coriander leaves, finely chopped

2–3 tablespoons water

oil, for greasing

butter, for folding and cooking

Put the dal in a saucepan with the salt, turmeric and measured water. Bring to the boil over a high heat, then reduce the heat and simmer for 15–20 minutes until the dal is tender. Set aside to cool.

To prepare the dough, combine the flour, salt, ground turmeric, chillies and chopped coriander leaves in a mixing bowl and mix well. Add the dal and stir well. Begin adding the measured water, 1 tablespoon at a time, adding just enough to bring the ingredients together into a soft dough. You don't want it to be sticky, so add as little water as you can. Put the dough in a lightly oiled bowl and cover the bowl with clingfilm. Leave to rest at room temperature for 30 minutes.

Divide the dough into 12 equal portions. Roll out 1 portion at a time into a 12–13cm (4½–5in) circle. Spread ½ teaspoon butter on it. Roll up the circle into a long cylinder, then twist the roll into a coil and roll it out again to a 15cm (6in) circle. Cook the parathas on a hot griddle or cast-iron frying pan for 2 minutes on each side. Then spread ½ teaspoon butter over each side and continue cooking on each side until golden. The dough will keep, refrigerated, in an airtight container for up to 4 days. Cook the parathas fresh when you need them.

In India there are many ways of making fenugreek paratha. Some like to knead fenugreek into the dough, others like to use a mixture of flours. My preference is to stuff the paratha with fenugreek *sabji* (a vegetable dish made with fenugreek). My mum makes these parathas very often in winter, the traditional season for fresh fenugreek. I absolutely love them and they are now my daughter's favourite type of paratha, too. Serve the hot, freshly cooked parathas with butter smoothed over, or with some raita and chutney on the side.

Fenugreek-stuffed paratha

Makes 9–10

For the filling

500g (1lb 2 oz) fresh fenugreek

1 tablespoon vegetable oil

2 potatoes, cut into 1cm (1/2in) dice

1/2 teaspoon salt

1/2 teaspoon chilli powder

For the dough

300g (10 1/2 oz) chapatti flour, plus extra for dusting

about 200ml (1/3 pint) water

vegetable oil, for frying

To make the filling, pull the leaves from the fenugreek and discard the thick stems. Chop the leaves roughly, then wash and drain thoroughly to remove all the excess water.

Heat the oil in a pan over a low heat. Add the fenugreek and potatoes, followed by the salt and chilli powder. Mix well, then cover and cook over a low heat for 20 minutes. Remove the lid, increase the heat to high and cook for a further 5 minutes to allow all the excess moisture to evaporate. Set aside to cool.

To make the dough, put the flour in a bowl and slowly add just enough of the measured water to bring the dough together – you might not need all the water or you might need a bit more. Knead the dough on a lightly floured surface for 5 minutes, then put it in a bowl, cover the bowl with clingfilm and leave to rest at room temperature for 15 minutes.

Divide the dough into 9–10 portions. Roll out 1 portion at a time into a 10cm (4in) circle. Spoon a little fenugreek *sabji* into the middle, then gather up the sides and seal together to enclose the *sabji* in a little round parcel. Press down on the parcel lightly, dust generously with flour and carefully roll it out into a 15cm (6in) circle.

Put a griddle or cast-iron frying pan over a medium heat and, once hot, lay a rolled paratha on it. Cook for 2 minutes on each side. Drizzle 1 teaspoon vegetable oil on each side of the paratha and cook each side for a few more seconds until golden. Serve hot. The dough and fenugreek *sabji* will keep, refrigerated, in airtight containers for up to 4 days. Cook the fresh paratha when you want them.

Fenugreek

Fresh fenugreek is a winter vegetable in India, where it is known as *methi*, and its dried leaves and seeds are used as herbs and spices throughout the rest of the year.

As you may have noticed from the recipes in this book, I love it. Mum's fenugreek-stuffed paratha is my all-time favourite fenugreek dish, but I am very fond of the dried leaves, too, adding them to curries, snacks, savoury doughs and pastries. Fenugreek gives a wonderful depth of flavour that is bitter and moreish, and it enhances the taste of other ingredients with which it is used.

India is the largest producer of fenugreek, with most of the crop coming from Rajasthan in the north, but it is grown throughout the subcontinent and Near East as well as in Spain, France, Ethiopia and Argentina.

Fresh fenugreek has oval- or slipper-shaped bright green leaves that are used very much like spinach or pea shoots (to which fenugreek is related). It can be cooked or eaten raw; tender parts of the stems can also be eaten.

Because of its high water content, fenugreek needs minimal water added during cooking; you will often see it simply washed, chopped and stirred into mixtures. It works particularly well with potatoes, chicken and lentils. Or try fenugreek in place of spinach in my pakora recipe (*see* page 165), as it is great with gram (chickpea) flour.

The sprouted seeds and tiny cress-like leaves do not have the same bitterness as the full-grown plant and can readily be eaten raw. In India they are made into pickles and raita, and added to rice dishes.

Dried leaves (*kashuri methi*) need only be crumbled into curries or bread doughs. I love them used in combination with carom, as in *papdi chaat* (*see* page 153), which is very popular in my home.

Fenugreek seeds are yellowy brown, very hard and have a cuboid shape rather like tiny dried corn kernels. They are larger than most other spice seeds, however, and need to be toasted carefully to bring out their best flavour; overheating makes them very bitter. Also, because fenugreek seeds are

strong, a little goes a long way. They are commonly used in commercial curry powders. Fenugreek seeds also feature in *panch phoran*, a favourite spice mix in Bangladesh, Eastern India and Nepal, and in *niter kibbeh*, Ethiopia's spiced clarified butter. You will find them in many Indian pickles, too.

Several clinical trials have shown that fenugreek seeds can improve symptoms of type 1 and type 2 diabetes. Many other health benefits are ascribed to them, such as improving colds, sore throats, arthritis, high cholesterol and kidney ailments. You can find fenugreek supplements in health food shops. Because fenugreek's health-giving properties continue to be researched, we are very likely to be talking more about it in future.

Recipes featuring fenugreek

Degi mirch chicken pie (*see* page 78)

Fenugreek papdi chaat (*see* page 153)

Coriander chicken parcels (*see* page 157)

Tomato and paneer loaf (*see* page 180)

Fenugreek-stuffed paratha (*see* page 207)

In India, these indulgent deep-fried flatbreads tend to be made for special occasions such as festivals, weddings and parties, or just on weekends. I think they're great for picnics and packed lunches, too. To make them, spinach purée is kneaded into plain puri dough to produce a lovely flavour and colour. Serve these puris with curries – *Aloo Sabji* (*see* page 217) is a perfect choice – or with some Cauliflower Pickle (*see* page 230).

Spinach puri

Serves 2

250g (9oz) spinach

500ml (18fl oz) boiling water

300g (10½oz) chapatti flour, plus extra for dusting

1 teaspoon salt

½ teaspoon chilli powder

sunflower oil, for deep-frying

Put the washed spinach leaves in a large pan and pour in the measured boiling water. Cover the pan with the lid and cook over a medium heat for 4 minutes, then drain thoroughly. Blend the spinach to a purée using a hand-held blender or food processor.

In a large bowl, mix the flour, salt and chilli powder together. Add the spinach purée and mix well, bringing the mixture together into a dough. If the mixture will not bind, add 2–3 tablespoons water – the dough should be soft but not wet. Knead it on a lightly floured surface for 2 minutes, then place it in a bowl, cover with clingfilm and leave it to rest at room temperature for 30 minutes.

Divide the dough into 18–20 portions and roll out each one into a 7.5cm (3in) circle.

Pour sunflower oil into a tall saucepan to a depth of one-third (or use a deep-fat fryer and follow the manufacturer's instructions). Heat the oil over a medium heat until a breadcrumb sizzles and turns brown when dropped into it. Once it is hot, fry 1 puri at a time for 1 minute on each side until golden brown. Drain on a plate lined with kitchen paper. Serve hot. The dough will keep, refrigerated, in an airtight container for up to 3 days. Fry fresh puri when you want them.

Warning: these super-soft wraps are so very quick and easy to make, the recipe could stop you settling for ready-made in future. Wraps are so handy for summer lunches, picnics, barbecues – and a lot more. To fill them, I like chilli chicken. There are many recipes for this, but my favourite is the way my mum makes it, so I'm giving you her version. When wrapping up the filling, don't forget to include chutney for depth of flavour, and some salad, for freshness.

Chilli chicken wraps

Serves 8

For the wraps

150g (5½oz) chapatti flour

100g (3½oz) plain flour, plus extra for dusting

½ teaspoon salt

30g (1oz) unsalted butter, softened, plus 2 teaspoons for spreading

about 140ml (4¾fl oz) water

For the filling

1 tablespoon green chilli sauce

2 tablespoons dark soy sauce

1 tablespoon cornflour

1 large egg, lightly beaten

1 teaspoon salt

5 tablespoons vegetable oil

300g (10½oz) boneless, skinless chicken breast, cut into thin, long strips

3 green chillies, quartered lengthways

2 onions, thinly sliced

To serve

Onion Chutney (*see* page 227)

watercress

To make the wraps, combine the flours, salt and butter in a bowl. Mix well, then slowly add the measured water, stirring to bring the dough together – you may not need all the water or you may need a bit more. Knead for 5 minutes on a lightly dusted work surface, then leave to rest at room temperature for 15 minutes in a bowl covered with clingfilm.

Divide the dough into 8 portions. Roll out 1 portion into a 15–18cm (6–7in) circle. Cook on a hot griddle or cast-iron frying pan over a medium heat for a couple of minutes on each side. Once cooked, spread ¼ teaspoon butter over 1 side. Repeat with the remaining dough portions, stacking the wraps up as you cook them. Wrap the stack in kitchen foil and set aside until you are ready to eat.

To make the filling, combine the chilli sauce, 1 tablespoon of the soy sauce, the cornflour, egg and ½ teaspoon of the salt in a bowl and mix well. Heat 4 tablespoons of the oil in a shallow pan. Working in batches, dip a few chicken strips in the chilli-egg mixture and fry in the oil over a medium heat for a couple of minutes on each side. Remove them to a plate lined with kitchen paper and set aside.

Use the same pan to cook the onions. Heat the remaining oil in it and add the chillies. Cook over a medium heat for 1 minute, then add the onions and cook over a low heat for 10–15 minutes until they have a little colour. Add the remaining salt and soy sauce, then return the chicken to the pan. Give it a good mix and set aside.

To assemble, take a wrap and spread it with Onion Chutney. Lay some chilli chicken in the middle and top with a few leaves of watercress. Roll it up and enjoy. The wraps will keep, covered in kitchen foil, for 2 days. The chicken will keep, refrigerated, in an airtight container for up to 4 days. Heat the wrap and chicken in a microwave oven before eating.

Plain naan is very easy and quick to make, but adding a filling turns it into a complete meal, such as this naan stuffed with minced chicken that has been cooked in a lovely blend of spices. It's delicious and is fairly healthy, too, as it is grilled rather than fried. Serve with any of the raitas on pages 232–235.

Chicken naan

Makes 9–10

For the dough

200g (7oz) plain flour

200g (7oz) chapatti flour, plus extra for dusting

1/2 teaspoon salt

1/2 teaspoon baking powder

2 garlic cloves, grated

100g (3 1/2 oz) natural yogurt

about 150ml (1/4 pint) water

oil, for greasing

butter, for brushing

For the filling

2 tablespoons vegetable oil

2 onions, finely chopped

2 garlic cloves, grated

2.5cm (1in) piece of fresh root ginger, peeled and grated

1 tomato, finely chopped

1 teaspoon salt

1 tablespoon garam masala

1 tablespoon ground coriander

1/2 teaspoon ground cinnamon

1/2 teaspoon ground cumin

1/2 teaspoon chilli powder

500g (1lb 2oz) minced chicken

To make the naan, combine the flours, salt, baking powder, garlic and yogurt in a bowl. Slowly add just enough of the measured water to bring the ingredients together into a dough – you might not need all the water or you may need a bit more. Knead the dough for 5 minutes on a lightly oiled surface. Put the dough in a lightly oiled bowl and cover with clingfilm. Leave to rest at room temperature for 30 minutes.

Meanwhile, prepare the filling. Heat the oil in a frying pan set over a low heat and add the onions. Cook for 2–5 minutes until the onions soften, then add the garlic and ginger and cook for another minute. Stir in the tomato, then the salt and all the spices. Cook for 1 minute. Add the minced chicken and cook for 5 minutes, stirring often, until the chicken is cooked through. Set aside to cool.

Divide the dough into 9–10 portions, then cut each portion in half. Roll out 1 piece on a lightly floured surface into an oval shape that is roughly 15cm (6in) long. Spoon 2 tablespoons of the chicken mixture into the centre. Roll out another piece of the dough into an oval of the same size as the first. Brush the edges with water, then lay it on top of the chicken-topped dough. Press around the sides to seal. Repeat with the remaining dough and filling.

Preheat the grill on a medium-high setting. Roll the sealed naan one last time and place them on a lightly floured baking tray. Grill for 2 minutes on each side, then brush well with butter. Serve hot. The dough and filling will keep, refrigerated, in airtight containers for up to 3 days. Roll fresh naan as desired.

Naan is traditionally made in clay ovens, so while it is very popular in India, especially in restaurants and at weddings, it is not often made at home. This naan stuffed with gingery cauliflower makes a complete meal, served with raita or chutney. I recommend Boondi Raita (*see* page 235).

Cauliflower-stuffed naan

Makes 12

For the dough

400g (14oz) plain flour, plus extra for dusting

1 teaspoon baking powder

1 teaspoon salt

3 tablespoons natural yogurt

about 160ml (5½fl oz) milk

oil, for greasing

butter, for brushing

For the filling

1 cauliflower, grated

1 teaspoon carom seeds

1 teaspoon salt

½ teaspoon chilli powder

1 teaspoon garam masala

2.5cm (1in) piece of fresh root ginger, peeled and grated

2 green chillies, finely chopped

handful of fresh coriander leaves, finely chopped

To make the dough, combine the flour, baking powder, salt and yogurt in a mixing bowl and slowly add just enough of the milk to bring the mixture together into a dough – you might not need all the milk or you may need a bit more. Knead the dough on a lightly oiled surface for 5 minutes until smooth. Place it in a lightly oiled bowl and cover the bowl with clingfilm. Leave to rest at room temperature for 15 minutes or so.

To make the filling, put the grated cauliflower in a bowl and add the remaining ingredients. Mix well and set aside.

Divide the dough into 12 equal portions. Roll out 1 portion at a time into a 10cm (4in) circle. Spoon 1½ tablespoons of the cauliflower mixture on to the centre of each circle. Gather the sides together and seal the cauliflower inside. Press down gently on the parcel and roll it out again into an oval shape that is roughly 15–18cm (6–7in) long. Place it on a lightly floured baking tray.

Preheat the grill on a medium–high setting. Cook the naan for 2–3 minutes on each side or until golden. Then brush ½ teaspoon butter over each naan and serve hot. The dough and filling will keep, refrigerated, in airtight containers, for up to 3 days. Roll and cook the naans fresh as you need them.

Once you realize how easy it is to make light, fluffy naan at home, you'll never buy the ready-made type again. With this basic technique you can try any number of toppings and stuffings. Here, I use garlic, coriander leaves and green chillies. The sharpness of garlic goes well with the fresh, woody notes of the coriander leaves, the coolness of which balances the chilli heat. A sprinkle of nigella seeds (*kalonji*) or black onion seeds gives a peppery finish. *Aloo sabji*, a simple dry potato curry, makes an excellent partner for the naan and turns this into a quick and delicious meal.

Garlic naan with aloo sabji

Serves 3–4

For the naan

300g (10½oz) plain flour, plus extra for dusting

½ teaspoon salt

½ teaspoon baking powder

3 tablespoons vegetable oil, plus extra for greasing

about 130–140ml (4¼–4¾fl oz) milk

butter, for brushing

For the *aloo sabji*

2 tablespoons vegetable oil

1 tablespoon cumin seeds

1 teaspoon salt

½ teaspoon chilli powder

1 teaspoon ground turmeric

1 teaspoon mango powder (*amchur*)

5 potatoes, boiled and roughly chopped into 2cm (¾in) cubes

For the topping

handful of nigella seeds (*kalonji*)

handful of finely chopped fresh coriander leaves

4 garlic cloves, finely chopped

4 green chillies, finely chopped

To make the naan, combine the flour, salt, baking powder and oil in a large mixing bowl. Slowly add just enough of the milk to bring the mixture together into a smooth, soft dough – you might not need all the milk or you may need a bit more. Remove the dough from the bowl and knead it on a lightly oiled work surface for 10 minutes. Put it into a lightly oiled bowl and cover the bowl with clingfilm. Leave to rest at room temperature for about 1 hour.

While the dough is resting, prepare the *sabji*. Put the oil in a pan set over a low heat and, once hot, add the cumin seeds. As soon as they start to change colour, add the salt and the remaining spices. Cook for 1 minute, then add the potatoes and mix well. Cook for 5 minutes over a low heat. Take the pan off the heat and set aside until the naans are ready.

Just before you are ready to eat, preheat the grill on its highest setting.

Divide the dough into 6 or 7 balls. Roll out the dough balls into any shape you like, such as round or oval, then gently prick them all over with a fork. Brush each naan with some water and sprinkle some nigella seeds, coriander, garlic and chillies over it. Place the naans on a lightly floured baking tray and grill for 1–2 minutes or until they start to change colour. Now turn them over and grill the other sides for less than 1 minute until, again, they start to change colour. Once cooked, brush each naan with butter and serve hot with the potato dish. Store the *aloo sabji* and the naan dough, refrigerated, in airtight containers: the *sabji* will keep for up to 4 days; the dough for up to 2 days. Leave the dough to stand at room temperature for 5 minutes before using. Reheat the *sabji* in a saucepan or microwave oven.

Accompaniments

This super-fresh chutney is really quick and easy to make and instantly adds flavour, colour and freshness to the meal or snacks it is paired with. It is versatile, too: it works beautifully with many starters and main meals, from papad and pakoras to grilled fish, lamb and chicken. A definite must-try.

Coriander and mint chutney

Makes 1 medium bowlful

75–100g (2³⁄₄oz–3¹⁄₂oz) fresh coriander, leaves picked

75–100g (2³⁄₄–3¹⁄₂oz) fresh mint, leaves picked

2–3 green chillies

juice of 1 lime

1 teaspoon salt

¹⁄₂ teaspoon granulated sugar

3 tablespoons water

Put all the ingredients in a blender or food processor and blend to a smooth paste. Serve straight away, or keep this chutney, refrigerated, in an airtight container for up to 5 days.

This chutney is not for the faint-hearted – it is extremely spicy. Yet it is one of my favourites and makes a delicious accompaniment to virtually any Indian dish. I would recommend that you try the recipe as suggested but if you wish you can regulate the heat by reducing the number of chillies. Don't be taken aback by the number of garlic cloves called for, as cooking these reduces their pungency. Try this and you'll be amazed that such an incredible taste can be created from so few ingredients.

Chilli and garlic chutney

Makes 1 medium bowlful

8–10 whole dried red chillies
15–20 garlic cloves
1 teaspoon salt
1 teaspoon granulated sugar
1 tablespoon coriander seeds
1 tablespoon cumin seeds
1 tablespoon vegetable oil

Soak the chillies in a bowl of water for 10–15 minutes, then drain them.

Put all the ingredients, except the oil, in a blender or food processor and blend to a smooth paste.

In a small pan, heat the oil over a low heat and add the chilli paste. Cook for 10 minutes until the garlic tastes cooked. Serve straight away, or keep this chutney, refrigerated, in an airtight container for up to 5 days.

This light and vibrant tomato chutney is inspired by the cuisine of Western India. The taste is sweet and sour, with a nice chilli kick. It is a great accompaniment to all sorts of foods and is also a fantastic way to use tomatoes when they are in season. This is beautifully refreshing for a hot summer's day and also very comforting with warm food in winter.

Tomato and garlic chutney

Makes 1 medium bowlful

8 tomatoes, roughly chopped
8 garlic cloves, roughly chopped
200ml (1/3 pint) water
1 tablespoon vegetable oil
pinch of asafoetida
1 teaspoon black mustard seeds
1 1/2 teaspoons salt
1 teaspoon chilli powder
big handful of fresh coriander leaves, finely chopped
1 1/2 teaspoons granulated sugar

Put the tomatoes, garlic and measured water in a saucepan. Bring to a simmer, then cover and cook over a low heat for 10–15 minutes. Take the pan off the heat and leave to cool a little. Transfer the contents of the pan to a blender and blend the mixture to a paste.

Heat the oil in a small pan set over a low heat. Add the asafoetida and, when it is fragrant, add the mustard seeds. When they begin to pop, add the tomato paste and salt. Cook over a low heat for 15–20 minutes until the mixture becomes a thick paste.

Add the chilli powder, coriander and sugar and mix well. Leave the chutney to cool a little before serving. This chutney will keep, refrigerated, in an airtight container for up to 3 days.

My mum makes this chutney a lot – the combination of flavours is fabulous. Mum usually roasts the peppers directly on the hob, but I prefer using the grill. Whatever method you decide on, the finished chutney is equally lovely eaten slightly warm when freshly made or chilled for eating later. Serve with simple crisps or any bread.

Red pepper and almond chutney

Makes 1 medium bowlful

2 red peppers

oil, for greasing

60g (2¼oz) ground almonds

1 teaspoon ground cumin

½ teaspoon salt

1 slice of brown bread, torn into pieces

juice of 1 lime

2 green chillies

4–5 tablespoons water

Roast the red peppers first. Preheat the grill on a high setting.

Cut the peppers in half, remove the seeds and core, then rub a little oil on the outer skins. Put the peppers, skin-side up, on a baking tray and grill for 5–10 minutes until the skin has blackened. Leave to cool for 5 minutes.

Remove the charred skin and put the flesh of the peppers in a food processor with all the remaining ingredients. Blitz until you have a fine paste. Serve straight away or chill until later. This chutney will keep, refrigerated, in an airtight container for up to 4 days.

Here is one of my mum's recipes that I've never played around with, as it is one of my favourites. She usually makes it as part of a South Indian meal. I like to serve it as an accompaniment to breads, or with crisps and canapés at parties – it always goes down a treat. The flavours contrast dramatically, yet come together to give a stunning result.

Coconut chutney

Makes 1 medium bowlful

1 fresh coconut, shelled and cut into small pieces

80g (2¾oz) roasted peanuts

2 green chillies, roughly chopped

1 teaspoon salt

150ml (¼ pint) water

5 tablespoons natural yogurt

1 tablespoon vegetable oil

1 teaspoon black mustard seeds

4 dried red chillies

10 fresh curry leaves

Combine the coconut, peanuts, green chillies, salt and measured water in a blender and blend until the mixture is fine. Add the yogurt and blend again to a smooth paste. Transfer the mixture to a bowl.

In a small pan, heat the oil over a low heat. Add the mustard seeds, dried red chillies and curry leaves and cook until the seeds begin to pop. Tip the tempered spices and the oil into the coconut chutney and mix well. This chutney will keep, refrigerated, in an airtight container for up to 2 days.

This is a staple chutney found in many Indian homes. It brings to life whatever it is served with. It's often found alongside snacks, such as samosas and *kachori*, and it is used in *chaat*, too.

Tamarind and date chutney

Makes 1 small bowlful

50g (1³/₄oz) tamarind paste

50g (1³/₄oz) pitted dates

50g (1³/₄oz) jaggery

350ml (12fl oz) water

¹/₂ teaspoon salt

1 teaspoon ground cumin

1 teaspoon chilli powder

1 teaspoon ground ginger

1 teaspoon dry-roasted fennel seeds, lightly crushed

Combine the tamarind, dates, jaggery and measured water in a saucepan and bring to the boil. Reduce the heat to low and cook for 15–20 minutes.

Strain the mixture through a fine sieve, ensuring that you press down well on all the ingredients to extract the maximum flavour.

Return the strained mixture to the pan, add the salt, cumin, chilli, ginger and fennel and cook for another 2 minutes. Leave to cool before use. This chutney will keep, refrigerated, in an airtight container for up to 14 days.

A fabulous combination of sweet jaggery, sour tamarind, sharp onions and spicy chillies, this chutney is a great one to serve with meals or as a dip for finger foods.

Onion chutney

Makes 1 medium bowlful

2 large onions, roughly chopped

3 dried red chillies

20g (³/₄oz) tamarind pulp

20g (³/₄oz) jaggery

1 teaspoon salt

300ml (¹/₂ pint) water

2 tablespoons vegetable oil

pinch of asafoetida

¹/₂ teaspoon black mustard seeds

¹/₂ teaspoon ground turmeric

10 curry leaves

In a food processor, blend the onions, chillies, tamarind, jaggery and salt with 100ml (3½fl oz) of the measured water to produce a smooth paste.

In a saucepan, heat the oil over a low heat and add the asafoetida. Once it is fragrant, add the mustard seeds, turmeric and curry leaves and cook for 1 minute. Stir in the onion paste and cook over a low heat for 10 minutes. Add 100ml (3½fl oz) more of the measured water, stir well and continue cooking for another 10 minutes. Once again, add the remaining measured water, mix well and cook for a final 10 minutes so that the onions are well cooked. Leave to cool. This chutney will keep, refrigerated, in an airtight container for up to 6 days.

Tamarind

Shady tamarind trees grow by the roadside in India as well as in many peoples' gardens. When I was a girl, there was a huge one on route to our school. Whenever it came into season, the tree would be loaded with long, brown pods and my sisters and I would stop and throw stones at it in order to break off the tamarind and eat the fruit, dipped in salt. I can still remember the taste of the very sharp, sour green flesh inside the crisp brown skin, although I haven't eaten tamarind so young and fresh since then.

As the tamarind fruit matures, the flesh becomes sweeter and darker in colour. It is possible to buy fresh ripened tamarind pods in the UK, but most supermarkets stock tamarind in dried blocks or as a paste.

I tend to use tamarind paste these days, as it is easy to buy and simply needs stirring into the other ingredients, but for some recipes, block tamarind is more suitable. To use it, break up the quantity of tamarind given in the recipe and put it in a non-metallic heatproof bowl. Cover with hot water (sometimes the recipe specifies an amount, sometimes not) and leave it to soak for a minimum of 20 minutes, stirring occasionally to encourage it to soften. Then press the tamarind and its soaking liquid through a sieve to make a thin paste or purée. The sieve will collect any seeds and tough fibres, which you should discard.

The sweet-sour aroma and flavour of tamarind, sometimes called the Indian date, is very refreshing. The tree, which probably hails from tropical Africa, is leguminous and therefore related to the beans, lentils and peanuts with which it goes so well. You may be enjoying it regularly without knowing, for tamarind is an important ingredient in British Worcestershire and brown sauces.

In India, tamarind is used in a wide range of curries and chutneys. Many households keep a jar of tamarind chutney in the refrigerator as a staple because it keeps for a long time and works with a huge variety of snacks, such as samosas and *kachori*. Tamarind chutney is a key component of *chaat*, the famous street food dish of potato, crisp fried *papdi*, yogurt sauce and lively flavourings, and *dahi vada*, lentil dumplings with spicy yogurt sauce and tamarind chutney.

Tamarind is particularly associated with South Indian cuisine, where it flavours drinks, rice and many curries. Next time you make a potato curry, try adding a dab of tamarind paste and finishing the dish with fresh coriander. I love using tamarind with lentils for a sweet-sour touch, and adding it to chutneys of other fruit or vegetables, where it can bring a great balance of flavour to very hot or very sweet mixtures.

Recipes featuring tamarind

Tamarind and date chutney (*see* page 227)

Onion chutney (*see* page 227)

Beetroot pickle (*see* page 230)

This wonderful pickle recipe comes from my mother's neighbour. The toasted sesame oil combined with sour tamarind and fiery chillies and garlic creates an extraordinarily complex flavour.

Beetroot pickle

Makes 1 jar

130ml (4¼fl oz) toasted sesame oil

15 garlic cloves, finely chopped

10 green chillies, finely chopped

2 beetroot (350g/12oz), grated

1 teaspoon salt

1 teaspoon chilli powder

1 tablespoon distilled malt vinegar

3 tablespoons tamarind paste

Heat 100ml (3½fl oz) of the sesame oil in a pan over a low heat. Add the garlic and green chillies and cook for 2 minutes. Take the pan off the heat and set aside to infuse.

In a large pan, heat the remaining 30ml (¾fl oz) oil. Add the grated beetroot and cook over a low heat for 5 minutes. Stir in the salt, chilli powder, vinegar and tamarind paste, then take the pan off the heat. Add the garlic-and-chilli-flavoured oil and mix well.

Transfer the mixture to sterilized jars and seal. Leave them in the sun or another warm place for 2–3 days to pickle. After that, store in a cool, dark place until needed. This pickle will keep for up to 5 weeks.

In India, cauliflowers are in season in winter. My mum used them every year to make this pickle. Although she would always make a good supply, it would be long gone by the following summer.

Cauliflower pickle

Makes 2 jars

1 cauliflower, cut into small florets

4 turnips, cut into 2.5cm (1in) cubes

150ml (¼ pint) mustard oil

25 garlic cloves, finely chopped

5cm (2in) piece fresh root ginger, peeled and chopped

1¼ tablespoons salt

1 tablespoon chilli powder

2 tablespoons garam masala

1½ tablespoons black mustard seeds, lightly crushed

2 tablespoons distilled malt vinegar

50g (1¾oz) jaggery

Wash the cauliflower florets and turnip pieces and drain thoroughly. Put them on a clean, dry tea towel to help remove all the water.

In a small pan, heat the oil, garlic and ginger over a low heat and cook for 6–8 minutes. Put the vegetables in a large bowl or pot and add the salt, chilli, garam masala and mustard seeds. Pour in the hot oil, including the garlic and ginger.

In a small pan, heat the vinegar and jaggery until the jaggery has melted. Pour this over the vegetables. Give the lot a good mix so that the spices and oil are well blended and the vegetables are thoroughly coated. Cover the pickle with a lid and place it in the sun for 1 week, giving it a good stir once a day. Transfer to sterilized jars and store in a cool, dark place. This pickle will keep for up to 2 months.

I like adding pulses to coleslaw to make the texture more interesting and the dish more substantial. This is a great accompaniment to many of the savoury bakes in this book.

Indian coleslaw

Makes 1 large bowlful

1/2 cabbage, thinly sliced

1 carrot, cut into batons

1/2 cucumber, cut into batons

4 spring onions, thinly sliced at an angle

400g (14oz) can five-bean salad, rinsed and drained

1 tablespoon olive oil

2 tablespoons lime juice

1/4 teaspoon salt

1/4 teaspoon ground black pepper

Put the cabbage, carrot, cucumber, spring onions and beans in a large bowl and mix well.

In a small bowl, whisk the olive oil, lime juice, salt and pepper together. Pour this over the salad, give it a good mix and serve immediately.

Here is my mum's recipe for cucumber raita (*see* photo, page 234). Raita is a well-known accompaniment to Indian meals. It balances spices and cools the palate. The freshness of cucumber here goes well with the natural sourness of yogurt. Cumin adds warmth and the mint helps to pull all the flavours together.

Cucumber raita

Makes 1 medium bowlful

250ml (9fl oz) natural yogurt

1/4 teaspoon salt

1/4 teaspoon chilli powder

1/2 teaspoon ground cumin

handful of mint leaves, finely chopped

1/2 cucumber

Put the yogurt, salt, chilli powder, cumin and mint in a bowl and mix together well.

Grate the cucumber and squeeze the excess water from the strands. Add the cucumber to the yogurt mixture and stir well. Serve straight away or serve chilled. This raita will keep, refrigerated, in an airtight container for up to 4 days.

When I was little, my mum made this dish all the time and now it is a firm favourite with my kids, too. *Boondi* are fried gram (chickpea) flour balls that are readily available in Asian shops. Some people soften the *boondi* in warm water before use, but I prefer to add them straight to the yogurt, as they don't take long to soften.

Boondi raita

Makes 1 medium bowlful

300ml (1/2 pint) natural yogurt
1/2 teaspoon salt
1 teaspoon ground cumin
1 green chilli, finely chopped
few mint leaves, finely chopped
100ml (31/2 fl oz) water
70g (21/2 oz) *boondi*

Combine all the ingredients in a bowl and mix together. Set aside for 20–30 minutes so that the *boondi* softens in the yogurt, then serve, or serve chilled. This raita will keep, refrigerated, in an airtight container for up to 4 days.

Bhindi or okra is a very popular green vegetable in Indian cuisine. I use it to make this lovely relish that goes very well with flatbreads, breads and small bites. The ground cumin and *amchur* (mango powder) give a great flavour boost to the crispy okra.

Bhindi raita

Makes 1 medium bowlful

150g (51/2 oz) okra
vegetable oil, for frying
1/4 teaspoon chilli powder
1/4 teaspoon ground cumin
1/4 teaspoon mango powder (*amchur*)
1/2 teaspoon salt
300ml (1/2 pint) natural yogurt

Wash and dry the okra, then slice them finely at an angle. Heat a little oil in a frying pan over a medium heat and, once hot, gently add the okra, ensuring that you don't overcrowd the pan – work in batches, if necessary, so that the okra is crunchy, not soggy. Cook for a couple of minutes until the okra is golden brown and crisp. Transfer to a plate lined with kitchen paper.

Put the okra in a bowl and sprinkle with the spices and 1/4 teaspoon of the salt. Give it a good stir and set aside.

When ready to eat, put the yogurt in a serving bowl, sprinkle with the remaining salt and mix well. Sprinkle the cooked okra on top and serve. This raita is best eaten straight away. It will keep, refrigerated, in an airtight container for up to 3 days, but the okra will not remain crisp.

Index

Acknowledgements

With many thanks to –

My Papa for always being so encouraging and supportive.

My Mummy for being the inspiration behind all my creativity.

My sisters Niti and Alpa for being my best friends and making us the best trio.

My friends for always being there.

My agent Stuart at Metrostar for believing in my ideas.

My publisher Octopus and commissioning editor Eleanor for the chance to make this book.

My photographer Nassima for bringing my imagination to life.

Leanne, Juliette, Caroline and Polly for putting so much effort into the book.

Jenny for helping me figure out my way with words.

My kids Sia and Yuv for all the love and cuddles.

And most importantly of all my husband Gaurav for all the love and support I could ever need.

641.5956   Makan, Chetna.
MAK

The cardamom trail.

JUN 0 2 2016